IN FOCUS

Strategies for
Academic Writers

MYRA SHULMAN

The University of Michigan Press

To K

Copyright © by the University of Michigan 2005
All rights reserved
ISBN 0-472-03075-2
Published in the United States of America by
The University of Michigan Press
Manufactured in the United States of America

2008   2007   2006   2005   4   3   2   1

Preface

The *In Focus* texts are aimed at high-intermediate to advanced students who would like to sharpen their writing skills. Native and non-native speakers who need a concise guide to effective writing will find the *In Focus* books useful. The purpose of *In Focus* is to offer writers suggestions on how to enjoy the writing process and improve the written product. While teaching both academic and business writing to university students and working professionals for many years, I have developed a practical approach that provides a structure for managing writing as well as strategies for achieving an effective style. The *In Focus* texts assume that students have successfully completed writing books that taught good paragraph writing and the process approach, introduced them to academic writing terms like *coherence* and *voice*, and familiarized them with the grammar and understanding of punctuation that produce good writing. These texts will build on those skills, offering specific practice in aspects of writing that will develop the skills needed to produce more advanced levels of academic and business writing.

In Focus: Strategies for Academic Writing incorporates the process approach to writing, with pre-writing analysis to clarify goals and post-writing editing and revision to refine style. The chapters contain short excerpts from professional authors as well as student-written models for the various genres. Most of the models are the final version of a document that has been through a number of drafts, so errors in grammar and mechanics have been corrected. These models give students practice in the critical evaluation of a document's strengths and weaknesses, which helps students become better editors of their own work and better peer editors of their classmates' work. After reading each model, students will discuss and practice specific strategies through a variety of tasks and then apply these strategies to their writing assignment. Students should be warned that the readings contain vocabulary with which they aren't familiar. Applying good vocabulary and reading skills will help students through the new vocabulary.

In Focus: Strategies for Academic Writers features academic writing assignments on the **paragraph, summary, essay, critical review, synthesis, argument,** and **research paper.** The text also encourages **response writing** in which students become accustomed to reacting to an article or idea and putting their reaction in writing, without revision. Thus, they gain confidence in their ability to articulate their ideas in written form.[1]

Chapters 1 and 2 lay the groundwork for the remaining chapters with an explanation of the **Focus Approach** and the **Power Writing Process.** When writers use the Focus Approach, a pre-writing technique, they clarify their thinking about the writing task as they consider these five factors:

Format
Organization
Content
Understanding
Style

The **Power Writing Process** enables writers to take control of the writing task by breaking down the project into five discrete steps. This application of a well-known time management technique (the "Swiss Cheese" method described by Alan Lakein[2]) makes any writing assignment manageable and less intimidating because it emphasizes working on one part of the writing project at a time. When doing a writing assignment, writers will find the task easier to complete if they follow these steps:

Prepare	**O**utline	**W**rite	**E**dit	**R**ewrite
Purpose	Thesis	Content	Clarity	Accuracy
Audience	Major points	Organization	Coherence	Readability
Goal	Minor points	Style	Conciseness	
	Supporting data		Precision	

[1] Response writing prepares students for the Next Generation TOEFL® (iBT®), which has two types of writing: a 30-minute opinion or preference (independent) essay and a 20-minute response to a reading and a lecture about the same topic (integrated essay). In 2005, the SAT® added a section called "Raw Writing" in which students submit a first draft without revising it. This section tests the ability to write quickly and concisely about a topic.

[2] Alan Lakein, *How to Get Control of Your Time and Your Life* (New York: Signet, 1974).

Of course, even a good textbook on writing may be of little use to those writers, both professional and amateur, who sometimes experience the inability to write, a problem called writer's block, or writing anxiety. Therefore, four techniques that can help students handle their writing anxiety are described and practiced in Chapter 3. These techniques prepare writers to cope with their anxiety in ways that minimize stress and maximize flexibility, thus building confidence and enhancing enjoyment of the writing process.

Chapter 4 addresses editing and proofreading. The act of writing demands the ability not only to think creatively but also to think critically and analytically, as an editor. Advanced grammar and proofreading tasks are included to serve as a reminder that proofreaders should be knowledgeable about the mechanics of writing. Chapter 5 on effective academic style follows the review of grammar since writers can best concentrate on sophisticated stylistic concerns after they have mastered the basics.

Chapters 6 through 12 provide guidelines and strategies for specific forms of academic writing, growing in complexity from the paragraph to the research paper. The final chapter, Your Authentic Voice, encourages students to trust their natural abilities, to explore their own authentic voices, and to enjoy the process of writing.

Six appendixes supplement the basic subjects of the text: Appendix A offers definitions of writing terms; Appendix B has examples of writing styles; Appendix C lists sentence connectors; Appendix D contains a step-by-step explanation of the Power Writing Process for each assignment; Appendix E has writing evaluation forms; and Appendix F offers tips on conducting Internet research.

A NOTE ON DOCUMENTATION FORMAT

When writers incorporate another person's words, facts, or ideas into their own writing, they must cite the source of this information. The three most commonly used documentation formats in academic writing are the APA (American Psychological Association), the MLA (Modern Language Association), and the Turabian/*Chicago Manual of Style*. Many of the writing assignments in this text require the use of outside sources and the documentation of these sources. The MLA in-text citation format is suggested for these assignments. However, students may prefer to use the documentation format required in their academic field.

The MLA citation format gives the author's last name and the page number in parentheses in the text. It lists all sources at the end of the paper as Works Cited, arranged alphabetically by the author's last name, or by title if no author is identified. The recommended text is the *MLA Handbook for Writers of Research Papers, 6th ed.* (New York: MLA, 2003).

The following websites contain information about the three major documentation formats:

- American Psychological Association: *www.apastyle.org* (contains guidelines and examples)
- Modern Language Association: *www.mla.org* (contains links but no guidelines and examples)
- Turabian/*Chicago Manual of Style*: *www.press.uchicago.edu* (contains FAQs and links but no guidelines and examples)

In addition, Duke University provides a Guide to Library Research with comprehensive information about citation rules under Citing Sources (Citing Sources and Avoiding Plagiarism: Documentation Guidelines) at *www.lib.duke.edu/libguide/.* For the rules on citation of electronic sources, see Citation Styles: Using MLA Style to Cite and Document Sources in Online! at *www.bedfordstmartins.com/online/cite5.html.*

ONLINE WRITING RESOURCES

This textbook contains models of writing assignments and short excerpts from published authors, but students can consult the following online resources for more writing guidelines and examples:

- Purdue University Online Writing Laboratory: *http://owl.english.purdue.edu/*
- The University of Illinois at Urbana-Champaign Writers' Workshop: *www.english.uiuc.edu/cws/wworkshop/*

Acknowledgments

I am deeply grateful to my editor, Kelly Sippell, who has a sharp eye for the right word and the best approach. Her moral support and practical guidance have been an inspiration to me.

My sincere thanks are offered to all the students whose writing appears in this text. They graciously allowed me to include their work so that others could benefit from their efforts and creativity. I also appreciate the wise advice and insightful comments from my colleagues and friends.

I want to thank my family for their infinite love, encouragement, and understanding: my husband K, brother David, and mother Deana were especially helpful in terms of being sensitive and thoughtful readers.

Like all such textbooks, this grew and developed from my personal teaching experience, reading, writing, and philosophy. Many contributed to its final form, and I thank everyone who offered suggestions for improvements, but I take responsibility for all errors.

Grateful acknowledgment is made to the following authors, publishers, journals, and individuals for permission to reprint previously published materials or their materials.

The McGraw-Hill Companies for "The Working Poor: We Can Do Better" in *Business Week*, May 31, 2004. Copyright © 2004 The McGraw-Hill Companies, Inc. Reprinted with permission.

Paul Gray for "Other People's Words" from *Smithsonian*, March 2002, copyright © 2002.

TIME, Inc., for "How I Caused That Story" by Doris Kearns Goodwin, February 24, 2002. Copyright © 2002 TIME, Inc. Reprinted with permission.

U.S. News & World Report, L.P., for "Learning to Live with Others," January 26, 2004, page 60. Copyright © 2004 *U.S. News & World Report*, L.P. Reprinted with permission.

Every effort has been made to contact the copyright holders for permission to reprint borrowed material. We regret any oversights that may have occurred and will rectify them in future printings.

Contents

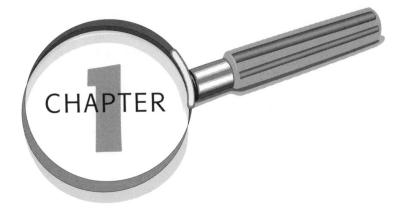

CHAPTER 1

The Focused Writer

EXCELLENCE IN WRITING

This textbook is intended for those who have a keen interest in writing well and want to improve the quality of their academic writing. It presents strategies as well as guidelines and models to help writers produce lucid and sound documents with relative ease and enjoyment of the creative process. Any piece of academic writing has to fulfill specific requirements and meet certain expectations, depending on the nature of the assignment. These requirements and expectations are different for documents produced by writers in business, engineering, law, medicine, or literature. And yet similarities exist. Good writing is good writing, whether we are talking about a business letter, memorandum, essay, research paper, or poem. It is characterized by an appropriate format, coherent organization, meaningful content, clarity of style, and an ability to get the message across to the reader in a memorable way.

There is no better way to learn to write well than to read examples of superior writing, including fiction and non-fiction, prose, and poetry. Although this may seem unusual, we will begin our discussion of academic writing by reading a poem, "The Red Wheelbarrow," by the 20th-century American poet William Carlos Williams (1883–1963).[1]

The Red Wheelbarrow
William Carlos Williams[2]

so much depends
upon

a red wheel
barrow

glazed with rain
water

beside the white
chickens.

[1] A wheelbarrow is a small, single-wheeled vehicle that is used for carrying small loads and is fitted with handles at the rear by which it can be pushed and guided. (*Merriam-Webster's Collegiate Dictionary*)
[2] William Carlos Williams, et al., *The Collected Poems of William Carlos Williams: 1909–1939*, vol. 1 (New York: New Directions, 1962), 224.

As William Strunk and E. B. White state in the well-known reference *The Elements of Style*:

> Vigorous writing is concise. A sentence should contain no unnecessary words, a paragraph no unnecessary sentences, for the same reason that a drawing should have no unnecessary lines and a machine no unnecessary parts. This requires not that the writer make all his sentences short, or that he avoid all detail and treat his subjects only in outline, but that every word tell.[3]

STRATEGIES: THE FOCUS APPROACH

The concept of writing with a well-defined purpose is conveyed by this book's title: *In Focus*. When you begin to write, think of yourself as a photographer, whose goal is to create a clearly focused photograph. To achieve this sharpness of focus, or mental clarity, you should prepare for writing by considering your purpose, audience, and goal in order to devise an effective writing strategy. As part of your strategy, ask yourself these questions about five significant aspects of a writing task.

• **F**ormat	What format should I use for this document?
• **O**rganization	How should I organize the information?
• **C**ontent	What type of information will I include?
• **U**nderstanding	What is my level of understanding of this topic?
• **S**tyle	What style would be appropriate for this document?

Just as a photographer takes some time to set up a shot, a writer needs time to think about the best framework for each document. This pre-writing analysis can be accomplished quickly by completing the Author's Framework Form (see page 4). Investing a few minutes in this activity will save you time during the writing process because you will have a focus for your project, an understanding of the parameters of the task ahead. It is especially helpful to put your purpose statement in writing.

---

[3] William Strunk, Jr., and E. B. White, *The Elements of Style*, 4th ed. (New York: Longman, 2000), 23. <u>Note:</u> The word *tell* in this sentence means be effective and expressive.

AUTHOR'S FRAMEWORK FORM

My purpose in writing this document is _____.

My audience for this document is _____.

My document is a/an _____ *(abstract, argument, critical review, essay, report, research paper, summary, synthesis).*

Format (What is the best length and visual design for this task?)

Number of pages	_____
Number of paragraphs	_____
Number of words	_____
Font type and size	_____
Spacing	_____
Margins	_____
Graphic aids	_____

Organization (How will I organize the material?)
Deductive (main idea at the beginning)
Inductive (main idea at the end)
Deductive-Restatement (main idea at the beginning and at the end)

Content (What type of content will I use?)
Personal
Impersonal
Research-based
Experience-based
Citation of sources
No citation of sources

Understanding (What is my level of understanding of the topic?)
High
Medium
Low

Style (What style would be appropriate for my purpose and audience?)
Objective
Subjective
Formal
Informal
Technical
Non-technical

As you read the following explanations, you will see that the factors involved in your pre-writing analysis are interrelated, and each affects the other.

Format

The first decision a writer has to make concerns the **format** of the document. This involves consideration of the appropriate length and graphic design in terms of font type and size, margins, spacing, headings, and visual aids. It is also important that the format remain the same throughout the document; in other words, it must be consistent. An appealing format is a crucial element in determining the impact of a document because it increases readability.

Organization

While the overall **organization** of a document should be linear, with ideas arranged in logical order, writers have a choice between a **deductive** (direct) or an **inductive** (indirect) pattern. In the United States, most readers want to know the main idea of a document right away. Therefore, writers usually choose deductive organization: They present the thesis or main idea at the beginning of the document, in paragraph one or two of the introduction.

They may also choose **deductive restatement,** with the main idea repeated in the conclusion. However, inductive organization, in which the thesis or main idea is presented at the end of the paper, is used less often in academic writing. Situations that require an indirect approach include a business letter or memorandum containing bad news or a scientific study with a controversial or complex subject.

Having chosen either deductive or inductive as your organizing principle, you must then decide which basic rhetorical pattern best matches your content. You can structure your document according to analysis, argument, cause-effect, chronology, classification, comparison-contrast, definition, description, enumeration, examples, problem-solution, process, or a combination of these patterns. Knowing in advance which structure you plan to use helps you impose order on your material in the early stages of writing.

Content

Content is the essence of any written product, so a writer must carefully consider what to include and what to omit. The purpose and audience of a document determine its content. This can range from a description of personal experience to analysis of data based on research to justification for an argument, requiring the use of outside sources with accompanying citations.

The best documents present content that is substantive, meaningful, and relevant, thus educating readers and inspiring them to think about the topic from a new perspective. Since organizational structure and content are interrelated, good writers consider these issues simultaneously. In general, structure and content must be congruent, which means that they fit well together. In other words, the content has been presented within the appropriate structure.

Understanding

Even though **understanding** of a topic is essential, sometimes writers have little if any knowledge of their topic and must do reading and research to be able to write about it. Before you begin to write, it is helpful to assess how much you know about the assigned or chosen topic so that you can plan how much time you will need to read up on the subject and understand the information so you can write about it. Good writing depends on an in-depth understanding of the topic, with content that is substantive and meaningful, not superficial. Also, having extensive knowledge of a subject increases your ability to write with specificity, not in generalities.

Style

Style is a choice, but it is also an inherent part of every writer's technique. All writers have their own unique writing voices, their own manner of expression. In addition, effective writers are in control of their styles and are able to adapt them to the purpose and audience so that the style is appropriate for the writing task. For example, an academic style is suited to essays, critical reviews, syntheses, arguments, and research papers. A business style is used for documents such as letters, memorandums, reports, resumes, proposals, and business plans.

In this text, *academic style* refers to the style of documents written for academic purposes, and it is characterized by varying degrees of objectivity, formality, and technical or scholarly language. In fact, style is a continuum ranging from extreme objectivity at one end to extreme subjectivity at the other. Although we can discuss the term *academic style* in general, such a style differs from one academic discipline to another. A style that is considered appropriate in the field of literature may be quite different from the preferred academic style in the field of information technology. Style also differs from one assignment to another. A short report would be less formal and contain less technical language than a lengthy research paper. An e-mail response to questions that an instructor posted on a course discussion board would be even less formal. (See Chapter 5, Effective Style, and Appendix B, Examples of Writing Styles.)

EVALUATION: "MY ACADEMIC AND PROFESSIONAL ACHIEVEMENTS"

After reviewing the completed Author's Framework Form (page 8), read the essay "My Academic and Professional Achievements" that begin on page 9, which is based on the form. This essay went through several drafts and was written by a student at the advanced level. Discuss the essay with your classmates, and evaluate it according to these criteria.

ESSAY EVALUATION

	Excellent +	Satisfactory √	Unsatisfactory –
Format	Appropriate and consistent presentation on the page		_____
Organization	Logical and coherent development of ideas		_____
Content	Substantive, meaningful, relevant discussion of topic		_____
Understanding	Extensive knowledge of the topic		_____
Style	Authentic writer's voice and effective style		_____

MODEL AUTHOR'S FRAMEWORK FORM

My purpose in writing this document is <u>to describe and analyze my personal academic and professional achievements and my future plans.</u>

My audience for this document is <u>my instructor and classmates.</u>

My document is <u>an essay</u>.

Format (What is the best length and visual design for this task?)

Number of pages	<u>2</u>
Number of paragraphs	<u>6</u>
Number of words	<u>600</u>
Font type and size	<u>Times Roman 12 point</u>
Spacing	<u>double space</u>
Margins	<u>1 inch</u>
Graphic aids	<u>personal photograph (not included)</u>

Organization (How will I organize the material?)
Deductive (direct)
Inductive (indirect)
<u>Deductive-Restatement</u>

Content (What type of content will I use?)
<u>Personal</u>
Impersonal
Research-based
<u>Experience-based</u>
Citation of sources
<u>No citation of sources</u>

Understanding (What is my level of understanding of the topic?)
<u>High</u>
Medium
Low

Style (What style would be appropriate for my purpose and audience?)
Objective
<u>Subjective</u>
Formal
<u>Informal</u>
Technical
<u>Non-technical</u>

Essay

My Academic and Professional Achievements

Tzu-Jian Hsu

I am the eldest child in my family and was born in Hsinchu city in Taiwan. My father, who used to be a teacher in junior high school, retired three years ago. My mother is an energetic homemaker, and my younger sister is working in the United States in a non-profit organization. I grew up in a harmonious family and was lucky to have a joyful childhood. However, I was a studious child and preferred reading books to playing or watching television. Most of all, I enjoyed going to school and being exposed to new ideas.

When I entered college, I chose industrial management as my major. This major equipped me not only to understand concepts about industry and business but also to develop my problem-solving ability. It emphasized system planning in order to make the production process smooth and efficient. Thus, I became knowledgeable about how industrial systems worked and could apply these concepts to the long-term planning of production and material management. In many courses, we were divided into teams when working on assignments, and I often assumed responsibility for project coordination, with a focus on developing team spirit.

I enlisted as a soldier in the Taiwan Air Force to complete my compulsory military service after graduating from college. At first, I faced many obstacles because of my unfamiliarity with military life, but I overcame these obstacles through cooperation with my colleagues in performing military duties. Besides the standard air force training, I received a license for driving trucks and had advanced computer training to meet the technological demands of my assignments. These experiences helped me to grow in maturity and discipline, which has been useful in my career.

After I left military service, I found employment in a bank as a teller. Surprisingly, it was a demanding job with minimum supervision; in fact, I took the initiative to implement a project to review the banking procedures done by tellers. As I accumulated practical knowledge and real-life experience, my self-confidence grew. Moreover, I acquired an understanding of the meaning of responsibility, respect, and reliability from my interactions with customers. These valuable interactions gave me the motivation and energy I needed to pursue my professional goals in a new direction.

Even though my education, military service, and work in a bank provided me with a great deal of practical knowledge, I realized I wanted to change my profession and get a master's degree in systems engineering. Because I hoped to attend graduate school in the United States, I enrolled in Georgetown University for a one-semester intensive English course to enhance my English language competence. I needed this concentration on English to prepare for the TOEFL and GRE. After returning to Taiwan, I applied to several graduate schools with superior programs in engineering.

Of course, I will face challenges during my two years in graduate school because of language and cultural differences, but the strong support of my family and friends will help me keep my spirits up and focus on my studies. When I graduate with an MS in systems engineering and return to Taiwan, this degree will represent the greatest achievement in my life. With perseverance I believe that I can accomplish my future professional goals, and I am looking forward to the opportunity to combine all my life experiences so that I can contribute to Taiwan's economic growth. I also plan to continue my education because learning new skills and ideas is important to me.

ASSIGNMENT Personal Analytical Essay

Write an essay about your own academic and professional achievements and your plans for the future. Before beginning to write, think about your writing strategy and what you want to accomplish in this essay. Then fill out the Author's Framework Form on page 4 for this assignment, exchange forms with a classmate, and discuss the similarities and differences in the information on your forms. When you have completed the essay, share it with the class.

CHAPTER

2

The Power Writing Process

STRATEGIES

This chapter presents an overall approach to writing clear, coherent, and concise documents. Power Writing is a systematic method that encourages a writer to follow a precise and logical process by breaking the writing task into five manageable steps.

Prepare

Before starting any asignment take a few minutes to analyze the purpose of your writing, your audience, and your goal by completing the Author's Framework Form. What type of document are you writing? What do you want to accomplish? What format will you use? To whom are you writing? What does your audience know about your topic? What do you already know about the topic? You may have to do research and read outside sources.

Outline

Make an outline of the thesis (main idea) and major points your document will include. You can do this in several ways: Write a detailed formal outline, write a shorter informal outline with your ideas, or make a list of major points. (See Model Outline Worksheet on page 16.) Think of your outline as a road map that can guide you in the right direction so that you arrive at your destination efficiently. Outlining in advance of writing produces a more logical and coherent document. It also shortens the writing time.

Write

Write your document, starting at any point in the outline. Some writers prefer to start from the introduction and work straight through to the conclusion. Others prefer to write the introduction last after they have discussed the major points. Try various ways to discover which works best for you. Don't neglect to proofread your first draft. Using the spell check and grammar check functions of your software program to help you identify problems.

Edit

You should take a break before beginning the editing process—a few hours or, if possible, several days. This time away from your document will give you the necessary distance you need to be an objective editor of your own writing. Edit your document by considering three aspects: the content, the organization, and the style. Don't hesitate to make changes if they improve the rough draft.

Rewrite

The final step in the Power Writing Process is to rewrite the rough draft, incorporating the revisions and corrections you made in the editing stage. At this point, you should also proofread the document again, correcting any remaining errors in grammar and mechanics to ensure the accuracy and readability of your document. Your final draft should be clear, coherent, concise, and precise. All good writing involves rewriting, so do not neglect this important stage. At the same time, avoid getting caught in a cycle of endless rewrites. That is counterproductive because often an early draft can be superior to later drafts that have lost their original energy through overwriting.

DISCUSSION: "MY EXPERIENCE WITH CULTURE SHOCK"

After reviewing the Model Author's Framework Form on page 15 and the Model Outline Worksheet on page 16, read "My Experience with Culture Shock" (pages 17–18), which is based on these forms. Then discuss the essay with your classmates by answering these questions:

- How believable is the author's explanation of her culture shock?
- Did you have a similar experience with culture shock?
- What are the strengths and weaknesses of this essay?
- What do you like best about this essay?

MODEL AUTHOR'S FRAMEWORK FORM

My purpose in writing this document is <u>to analyze my experience with culture shock.</u>

My audience for this document is <u>my instructor and classmates.</u>

My document is a <u>personal analytical essay</u>.

Format (What is the best length and visual design for this task?)

Number of pages   <u>2</u>

Number of paragraphs   <u>5</u>

Number of words   <u>500</u>

Font type and size   <u>Times Roman 12 point</u>

Spacing   <u>double space</u>

Margins   <u>1 inch</u>

Graphic aids   <u>none</u>

Organization (How will I organize the material?)
Deductive (direct)
Inductive (indirect)
<u>Deductive-Restatement</u>

Content (What type of content will I use?)
<u>Personal</u>
Impersonal
Research-based
<u>Experience-based</u>
Citation of sources
<u>No citation of sources</u>

Understanding (What is my level of understanding of the topic?)
<u>High</u>
Medium
Low

Style (What style would be appropriate for my purpose and audience?)
Objective
<u>Subjective</u>
Formal
<u>Informal</u>
Technical
<u>Non-technical</u>

MODEL OUTLINE WORKSHEET

General topic: _My Experience with Culture Shock_

Purpose statement: _The purpose of this essay is to explain my problems with culture shock in the United States._

General method of organization (deductive or inductive): _deductive_

  I. Paragraph 1: Introduction
   Main idea of the communication (thesis)
   However, after about one month, culture shock affected me because I had trouble communicating in English, I couldn't adjust to American college life, and the liberal attitudes of Americans made me feel uncomfortable.

 II. Paragraph 2: Body
   A. Major point (aspect of main idea): _communication_
   B. Topic sentence: _One reason that I experienced culture shock was that I had trouble communicating with people who were speaking English, so I was lonely_
   C. Types of supporting data: _facts and examples_

III. Paragraph 3: Body
   A. Major point (aspect of main idea): _college life_
   B. Topic sentence: _The second cause of my culture shock was lack of adjustment to my new college life._
   C. Types of supporting data: _facts and examples_

 IV. Paragraph 4: Body
   A. Major point (aspect of main idea): _liberal Americans_
   B. Topic sentence: _Finally, North Americans appeared to be more liberal than Turkish people, which made me feel quite uncomfortable._
   C. Types of supporting data: _facts and examples_

  V. Paragraph 5: Conclusion
   A. Major point (restatement of main idea): _My cultural adjustment to life in Washington, DC_
   B. Topic sentence: _My cultural adjustment to life in Washington, DC, was a difficult challenge for me._
   C. Types of concluding data: _summary and prediction_

Essay Based on Outline Worksheet

My Experience with Culture Shock

I came to study in the United States in the fall of 2003 after graduating from my high school in Ankara, Turkey. I chose Washington, DC, having heard that the city was really beautiful, offered many cultural attractions, and had an international population. When I first arrived at Georgetown University, located in northwest Washington, I was excited and happy to be starting a new and independent life. However, after about one month, culture shock affected me because I had trouble communicating in English, I couldn't adjust to American college life, and the liberal attitudes of Americans made me feel uncomfortable.

One reason that I experienced culture shock was that I had trouble communicating with people who were speaking English, so I was lonely. I was like a fish out of water. Of course, I tried to speak English, but North Americans didn't seem to understand me, and I couldn't understand them because they spoke so fast. Also, during those first weeks, I never had the opportunity to meet any Turkish students, which caused another problem. I was all alone in an unfamiliar place where I had no friends who spoke my language.

The second cause of my culture shock was lack of adjustment to my new college life. I had a difficult time getting used to the academic environment and the educational system. The customs were much different from those in my country. For example, students sometimes talked with each other even when the professor was speaking, or they ate and drank in the classroom. Furthermore, students interrupted each other during the discussions and frequently asked the professor questions. They seemed in some cases almost to be in charge of the class. Indeed, they even called their professors by their first names. I wasn't used to such disrespectful and aggressive behavior.

Finally, most North Americans appeared to be more liberal than Turkish people, which made me feel quite uncomfortable. I could see this liberalism in the way many American students dressed, their behavior in public, and their topics of conversation. Concerning clothing, Turkish students, especially women, tend to dress conservatively, but American students wear all sorts of strange outfits. In public places, Turkish couples usually don't kiss or hug each other, and group conversations don't center on private issues. All these differences were shocking to me at first. Overall, I missed my country, and I wanted desperately to go back to see my family. I began to wonder if I would ever become comfortable living in the United States.

My cultural adjustment to life in Washington, DC, was a difficult challenge for me. Since I couldn't communicate well in English and I had no friends, I felt isolated and somewhat hostile. I was constantly criticizing life in the United States, from the weather to the food. Nevertheless, after the first semester, I started to forget about my family and friends in my country, made new friends from around the world, and got used to speaking English with everyone. I was also able to look back at my culture shock and see the humor in the situation. Most important, I was glad that I'd come to study in the United States and pleased with my accomplishments. Now I'm preparing to face reverse culture shock when I return to my country because I'm so accustomed to American culture.

Analysis of Structure

Working with a partner, analyze and evaluate the organizational structure of "My Experience with Culture Shock" by completing these tasks.

- Underline the thesis (main idea).
- Underline the topic sentences in each paragraph.
- Highlight the facts, statistics, examples, or quotations that support the topic sentences.
- Highlight the sentence connectors (transition words) that add coherence to the paragraphs.
- Examine the format (visual design) of the document. What do you notice?

Analysis of Style

Next, consider the style of this author and the readability of the essay. The best writing style is natural, clear, and concise, characteristics that improve the readability of a document. Furthermore, a review of a document's sentence connectors, pronouns, verbs, adjectives, adverbs, and contractions will indicate whether the author's style is subjective or objective, formal or informal, and technical or non-technical. (Chapter 5 contains a more extensive discussion of the characteristics of effective academic style, and Appendix B provides examples of various writing styles.)

Sentence Connectors

Sentence connectors add coherence to the paragraph and logical development to the essay as a whole. They can connect sentences within a paragraph and also act as signal words between paragraphs, delineating the major points of the document. Words such as *therefore* (result) and *nevertheless* (contrast) convey meaning to the reader while ensuring the smooth flow of ideas. Indeed, the use of sentence connectors has a positive impact on both the organization and style of a document, but when overused, connectors lose their natural quality.

Formal sentence connectors are conjunctive adverbs. They include *therefore, thus, as a result, nevertheless, however, in addition, furthermore, moreover, indeed, in fact, first, second, third, in conclusion, finally, on the other hand, in contrast, on the contrary, accordingly,* and *generally.*

Informal sentence connectors are coordinate or coordinating conjunctions. They include *and, but, for, as, so, yet, or,* and *nor.* (See Appendix C for a list of sentence connectors in English, their meaning, and punctuation rules.)

Pronouns

Analysis of the type of **pronouns** in a document can be instructive. The choice of a large number of first-person pronouns (*I, we*) produces a subjective style and personal tone, as does the use of second-person pronouns (*you*). Use of mostly third-person pronouns (*he, she, it, they*) results in an impersonal tone and objective style, and thus may lend an air of formality to the document.

As a grammar point, when analyzing pronouns, check that the pronoun matches the **referent** (the noun to which the pronoun refers) in terms of being singular or plural.

> **Example:** Although the decision Antonio made to pursue a career in business was based on several factors, **it (the decision)** was mainly determined by the strength of his communicative skills and his technology skills. These skills are his greatest assets, and **they (skills)** will ensure his success in international business.

Verb Choice

Verb choice, more than any other stylistic decision, conveys the level of formality of a document. The difference between *examine* and *look over* or *consider* and *think about* is great. It is also effective to write in the active voice, rather than the passive, using strong verbs that can add energy to writing. In many ways, the verb is the heart of a sentence, so you can check the clarity of your writing by analyzing your verbs. Have you chosen active, concrete, energetic verbs or passive, abstract, weak verbs?

Adjectives and Adverbs

Adjective and adverbs produce a colorful and dramatic style and tone, but too many can create an effect that is not appropriate for academic writing, which tends to have a balanced, understated tone. On the other hand, writing that has no adjectives or adverbs is boring and lacks specificity. The best documents are characterized by a judicious use of adjectives and adverbs that show variety in word choice. In general, avoid overused adjectives and adverbs such as *nice, good, bad, pretty,* and *very.*

Contractions

Contractions are not a characteristic of a formal writing style but are acceptable in an informal style. Read these sentences aloud, and listen to the difference in tone.

Informal: *I'll try to be on time to the meeting, but I can't promise I'll make it.*

Formal: *I will try to be on time to the meeting, but I cannot promise that I will make it.*

Evaluation of Style

In order to evaluate the author's style in "My Experience with Culture Shock," discuss the word choice in this essay by considering the following with your classmates:

- sentence connectors (transition words)
- pronouns
- verbs
- adjectives and adverbs
- contractions

After your discussion, circle the words on this list that describe the style of this writer.

subjective	formal	technical
objective	informal	non-technical

ASSIGNMENT Personal Analytical Essay

Write an essay describing your experience with culture shock when you lived in a foreign country. Use the Power Writing Process.

- **Prepare:** Fill out the Author's Framework Form on page 23.
- **Outline:** Use the Outline Worksheet on page 24 to make an outline of your content.
- **Write:** Develop your first draft, following the organization of your outline.
- **Edit:** Examine the strengths and weaknesses of the content, organization, and style.
- **Rewrite:** Write your essay again, incorporating your revisions and corrections.

Outline Worksheet

The Outline Worksheet on page 24 makes the process of writing more efficient. Begin with your general topic and your purpose before writing the main idea (thesis). Next list the major points in just a few words, and create topic sentences from these points. The supporting data to develop each body paragraph include facts, statistics, examples, or quotations from outside sources. The concluding data can be a brief summary, a prediction about the future, a solution to a problem, or a relevant quotation.

AUTHOR'S FRAMEWORK FORM

My purpose in writing this document is _____.

My audience for this document is _____.

My document is a/an _____ *(abstract, argument, critical review, essay, report, research paper, summary, synthesis).*

Format (What is the best length and visual design for this task?)

Number of pages _____

Number of paragraphs _____

Number of words _____

Font type and size _____

Spacing _____

Margins _____

Graphic aids _____

Organization (How will I organize the material?)
Deductive (main idea at the beginning)
Inductive (main idea at the end)
Deductive-Restatement (main idea at the beginning and at the end)

Content (What type of content will I use?)
Personal
Impersonal
Research-based
Experience-based
Citation of sources
No citation of sources

Understanding (What is my level of understanding of the topic?)
High
Medium
Low

Style (What style would be appropriate for my purpose and audience?)
Objective
Subjective
Formal
Informal
Technical
Non-technical

OUTLINE WORKSHEET

General topic: _____

Purpose statement: _____

_____

General method of organization (deductive or inductive): _____

I. Paragraph 1: Introduction
   Main idea of the communication (thesis)

   _____

   _____

   _____

II. Paragraph 2: Body
   A. Major point (aspect of main idea): _____
   B. Topic sentence: _____

   _____

   C. Types of supporting data:_____

III. Paragraph 3: Body
   A. Major point (aspect of main idea): _____
   B. Topic sentence: _____

   _____

   C. Types of supporting data:_____

IV. Paragraph 4: Body
   A. Major point (aspect of main idea): _____
   B. Topic sentence: _____

   _____

   C. Types of supporting data:_____

V. Paragraph 5: Conclusion
   A. Major point (restatement of main idea): _____

   _____

   B. Topic sentence: _____

   _____

   C. Types of supporting data:_____

Peer Critique: First Draft

After you have finished your first draft, exchange papers with a classmate and evaluate the essays by considering these characteristics of effective documents.

- The introduction ends with a clear thesis statement.
- The body paragraphs support the thesis statement (main idea).
- Each body paragraph has a topic sentence related to the thesis.
- The remaining sentences in each paragraph support the topic sentence.
- Facts, statistics, examples, or quotations are used to expand on the topic sentence.
- The paragraphs are unified, coherent, and appropriate in length.
- Sentence connectors add coherence within and between the paragraphs.
- Verbs, adjectives, and adverbs are used effectively.
- The conclusion is meaningful and logical.
- The style of the document is appropriate and readable.

Now rewrite your first draft, incorporating the revisions and corrections you wish to make.

WRITING ANXIETY QUESTIONNAIRE

Before experimenting with the methods that will help overcome writing anxiety, also known as writer's block, you might want to discover whether you suffer from this common problem. Read these statements, and select the appropriate number that best reflects your feelings.

1 = strongly disagree   2 = disagree   3 = neutral   4 = agree   5 = strongly agree

1. I am not worried about my writing skills. _____

2. I do not have a problem completing writing tasks. _____

3. I don't postpone doing writing assignments. _____

4. Getting a writing assignment does not make me feel anxious. _____

5. I am generally confident about my writing skills. _____

6. I usually enjoy the writing process. _____

7. Taking a course in writing would be an enjoyable experience. _____

8. My knowledge of English grammar and mechanics is excellent. _____

9. My writing is logically organized and coherent. _____

10. My vocabulary in English is extensive. _____

11. My writing style is effective. _____

12. I have a good understanding of how to create an effective document. _____

Score: 12–24 = You have a serious case of writing anxiety.

25–36 = You have a moderate case of writing anxiety.

37–48 = You have confidence in your writing.

49–60 = You enjoy writing.

Timed Writing

Think about a current problem or challenge in your life, and write about this issue without stopping for at least ten minutes. The goal is to continue to write and express your thoughts. Do not worry about grammar, punctuation, or the other mechanics of writing. Just practice turning your ideas into written form. You may be surprised to discover that a solution to your problem has emerged while you are writing.

Writer's Journal

Keep a journal, sometimes called a diary. Write in it every day or every night. This journal should be more than a listing of your daily activities; it should be a chance to express your emotions and concerns—a record of your private thoughts, hopes, dreams, plans, ideas, and memories. What, when, and how much you choose to write are up to you, but don't forget to write on a regular basis. Once you get in the habit of writing in your journal, you will not feel right if you don't make your daily entry.

Response Writing

Read an article from an online news source or the newspaper, or choose a literary work, such as a poem or a short story. After you finish reading, write a personal response in one or two paragraphs, without taking time to revise. Explain how you felt about this article or literary work, whether you agreed with the author's ideas, or what the most memorable aspect was. Ask questions about what you read. Do not worry about grammar, punctuation, or the other mechanics of writing. The important point of this activity is to respond to the reading while it is still fresh in your mind. Practice in response writing will sharpen your ability to organize your thoughts quickly and write them down concisely.

 TASK   Freewriting—Time

The purpose of this type of writing task is to enhance your writing skills by freeing you from the numerous restrictions on format, content, organization, and style that writers usually have to accept. If you practice freewriting on a daily basis, you will gain confidence in your writing and improve your ability to transform thoughts from your mind into words on the page.

Write the word *time* at the top of your page, and do freewriting for ten minutes. Just relax and let free association guide your thinking and writing. While you are writing, do not worry about grammar, punctuation, and the other mechanics of writing. At the end of ten minutes, read what you have written and circle any one word (but not the word *time*) that you have used more than once in your freewriting. Write that circled word at the top of a second page, and then write for ten more minutes of freewriting. When you are finished, share your writing with your classmates, and discuss your reaction to this activity with the class.

How did you enjoy this freewriting?

How easy was it for you to keep writing for ten minutes? And then for another ten minutes?

Are you pleased with what you wrote?

 TASK **Response Writing—"Marriage Past and Present"**

Read the passage about marriage on page 31. After thinking about the ideas in the paragraphs, write a response to the ideas. While you are writing, do not worry about grammar, punctuation, and the other mechanics of writing. The purpose of this activity is to give you practice in communicating your thoughts in written form in a spontaneous manner, without allowing for any revision. When you have completed your response, share it with the class by reading it aloud.

MARRIAGE PAST AND PRESENT

The convention of marriage began many centuries ago as a way to protect the wealth of families. In the earliest conception of marriage, men and women from the upper classes married each other as a means of keeping their financial assets and real estate within their families. Besides the expansion of family property, people married to build political alliances or to strengthen social obligations, such as providing a stable environment for the raising of children. Today, these traditional purposes of marriage have disappeared to a large extent. If a man and a woman decide to become husband and wife, it is usually unrelated to considerations of wealth or the stability of society. Most people marry because of a desire for both romantic love and long-term companionship.

Also, the definition of marriage is undergoing a revision in light of the laws in Massachusetts, the Netherlands, Belgium, and three Canadian provinces that allow men to marry men and women to marry women. These laws give gay couples "not only the rights and obligations of marriage but the word itself."[1] Such same-sex marriages have led to a "struggle over the meaning and purpose of matrimony."[2] It is possible that these marriages will transform and liberalize the traditional concept of marriage by challenging the idea that only a man and a woman can wed. Certainly, the definition of marriage will continue to be debated around the world.

Response . . . .

_____

_____

_____

_____

_____

_____

_____

_____

_____

_____

_____

[1] Adam Haslett, "Love Supreme: Gay Nuptials and the Making of Modern Marriage," *The New Yorker*, May 31, 2004, 76.

[2] Ibid., 76.

TASK **Response Writing—George Bernard Shaw Quotation**

What is your opinion on the institution of marriage? Do the advantages outweigh the disadvantages? What sacrifices do you think people make when they marry? In this quotation, the 20th-century British author George Bernard Shaw makes a statement about marriage. After thinking about Shaw's quotation, write a response.

While you are writing, do not worry about grammar, punctuation, and the other mechanics of writing. The purpose of this activity is to give you practice in communicating your thoughts in written form in a spontaneous manner, without allowing for any revision. When you have completed your response, share it with the class by reading it aloud.

"The greatest sacrifice in marriage is the sacrifice of the adventurous attitude toward life: the being settled."[3]

Response . . . .

_____

_____

_____

_____

_____

_____

_____

_____

_____

[3] George Bernard Shaw, Preface to _Androcles and the Lion,_ 1912. <u>Note:</u> A _sacrifice_ is something a person gives up. _Being settled_ means living according to a regular routine and an established pattern.

CHAPTER **4**

Skillful Proofreading and Editing

Proofreading and editing are two separate cognitive processes, and they involve different aspects of a document and different critical thinking skills. Therefore, you should not proofread and edit a document simultaneously. When you are **proofreading,** you have to identify and correct errors in the grammar and mechanics (punctuation, capitalization, spelling, abbreviations, use of numbers) of your paper. You also have to determine whether the format, the visual design of a document, is appropriate and consistent. Being a good proofreader requires precision, patience, and knowledge of English grammar and mechanics. Your final goal is to ensure the accuracy of the entire document.

When you are **editing,** you have to consider the content, organization, and style of your paper and make revisions that improve these aspects. Being a good editor requires a strong foundation in all the interrelated skills of writing because you are evaluating the overall quality and impact of a document. You should proofread and edit your first draft, rewrite it with necessary changes, and proofread your final draft before handing it in.

Having edited and proofread your document, you are helping your reader to interpret and understand your message easily, which means that your document has **readability.** This is a characteristic of excellent writing that results from producing a document that is clear, coherent, concise, and precise. If the language of your document is unclear, incoherent, redundant, and imprecise, your reader may not understand the message. This is a failure of communication.

--- **STRATEGIES** ---

Proofreading Principles

Grammar: The document is written in standard English grammar.

Mechanics: The mechanics (punctuation, capitalization, spelling, abbreviations, number use) are correct.

Format: The format is appropriate and consistent, according to the standard visual design for each type of document, whether an essay or a business letter.

Editing Principles

Content: The content of a document is substantive, meaningful, and relevant.
Organization: The organization is logical and coherent.
Style: The style is clear, coherent, concise, and precise, and adapted to the
purpose and audience.

Readability

Readability is a characteristic that refers to how easily a reader can understand your message. A document that is readable is appropriate in style, consistent in tone, accurate in content, and logical in organization. Of course, grammar and punctuation errors detract from readability.

Readability results from a variety of factors including how many long sentences and multi-syllable words you have used. Writing with short, concrete words rather than complex, abstract words and with simple, complex, or compound sentences rather than long compound-complex sentences will increase the readability of any document. The length of paragraphs also influences readability. Readers sometime become discouraged when they are faced with extremely long paragraphs. They appreciate taking in information in small chunks.

The readability formula is part of many software grammar check programs, and it is a good tool to use after you have completed your first draft. The final number that results from applying the readability formula is equal to a grade level and tells you how difficult your document is to read. Most readability experts suggest that you aim for the number 12 (12th grade) or even lower to ensure the readability of your document. (You can apply the Flesch-Kincaid Reading Level analysis to your writing by using the grammar check in Microsoft Word's software program.)

Readability Analysis

Using the readability formula, analyze the readability of the paragraph on page 36, which is from the essay "My Experience with Culture Shock." The paragraph has 100 words.

Readability Formula[1]

1. Count 100 words of a document.
2. Count the number of sentences in the section of 100 words.
3. Divide the number of words by the number of sentences.
4. Count the number of words with three or more syllables. Do not include capitalized words or verbs.
5. Add the result of #3 and #4 together.
6. Multiply the result of #5 by 0.4 (the readability factor).
7. The result is the readability level of the document. The number is equal to the number of years of education a person needs to understand the document.

Example: 20 (average number of words per sentence)
         $\underline{+10}$ (number of multi-syllable words)
         $30 \times 0.4 = 12$ (12th grade readability level)

My Experience with Culture Shock

I came to study in the United States in the fall of 2003 after graduating from my high school in Ankara, Turkey. I chose Washington, DC, having heard that the city was really beautiful, offered many cultural attractions, and had an international population. When I first arrived at Georgetown University, located in northwest Washington, I was excited and happy to be starting a new and independent life. However, after about one month, culture shock affected me because I had trouble communicating in English, I couldn't adjust to American college life, and the liberal attitudes of Americans made me feel uncomfortable.

---

[1] Robert Gunning and Douglas Mueller, *How to Take the Fog Out of Writing* (Chicago: The Dartnell Corporation, 1981), 9–11.

CONCISE GRAMMAR REVIEW

Writers must be familiar with the rules and conventions of English grammar and punctuation in order to proofread a document skillfully. To evaluate your knowledge of standard English grammar, read the brief explanation that follows of major grammar points and the examples of the most common errors made by writers. If you cannot correct these basic errors, you may need a comprehensive review of English grammar and punctuation. There are many books that contain rules and examples, such as *The Elements of Style, 4th edition*, by Strunk and White, which is a popular and useful reference on writing. You can also access websites that provide information on this topic. These are two of the best sites:

- Purdue University Online Writing Laboratory: *http://owl.english. purdue.edu/*
- The University of Illinois at Urbana-Champaign Writers' Workshop: *www.english.uiuc.edu/cws/wworkshop/*

Common Grammar Problems

After reviewing the grammar points, read the sentences and correct the underlined errors in these sentences.

Subject-verb agreement: A subject must agree with its verb in number. A singular subject needs a singular verb. A plural subject needs a plural verb.

Example of error: The questions on the history exam about the causes of the Civil War <u>was</u> difficult.

Pronoun-referent number agreement: A pronoun must agree in number with its referent, the noun to which it refers. A singular pronoun refers to a singular noun. A plural pronoun refers to a plural noun. (Note that gender-neutral language requires the words *he or she* and *his or her,* instead of *he* and *his.*)

Example of error: Each student brought <u>their</u> laptop computer to the conference.

Dangling modifier: A dangling modifier is a phrase that has no logical subject.

Example of error: <u>Having done all the interviews,</u> the data had to be analyzed.

Misplaced modifier: A misplaced modifier is a word, phrase, or clause that is not located next to the word it is modifying.

Example of error: He brought the negotiating skills book back to the library <u>that the teacher had assigned.</u>

Preposition usage: A preposition is a function word that generally connects a noun or pronoun to another element of the sentence. *(She threw the ball <u>over</u> the wall.)* It is also used with verbs to form two-word (or phrasal) verbs, such as *get off* the bus. Using prepositions correctly is a challenge to almost everyone, but you can do it. Try to read many books, magazines, and newspapers in English and listen to the spoken language. Eventually you will succeed in mastering prepositions.

Example of error: The project leader asked us to think <u>on</u> what we planned to include <u>on</u> the report <u>of</u> immigration.

Article usage: Articles are used with nouns to limit or modify their meaning. Although English has only three articles, *a, an,* and *the,* their usage is quite complicated. The indefinite articles *a* and *an* are used to describe a countable noun in general. *(I ate an apple.)* The definite article *the* is used to specify a particular noun, whether countable or uncountable. *(The apple that I ate was delicious. The snow that was predicted did not arrive.)*

Example of error: Eating <u>the</u> orange everyday and drinking <u>a</u> milk will keep you healthy.

Verb tenses: A verb functions to express an action, an occurrence, or a state of being. Since verbs are the heart of a sentence, writers who can use verb tenses correctly are able to convey their meaning precisely. The English language has simple, perfect, and progressive verb tenses, and writers should be familiar with the commonly used present, present perfect, past, past perfect, future, and future perfect tenses in particular, along with the progressive and conditional forms of these tenses.

Example of error: I <u>am wanting</u> to stay fit, so I <u>am deciding</u> to go to the gym every day.

Example of error: Before talking to her professor, Jane <u>has</u> carefully <u>read</u> the homework assignment.

Example of error: Juan Carlos will have <u>complete</u> his MBA by the time he gets married on June 16.

Example of error: I would transfer to a different school if I <u>was</u> you.

Parallelism: Similar ideas should be written in similar grammatical form. This technique can add to the effectiveness of your writing when you are using a series in a sentence, correlative conjunctions *(not only-but also, both-and, neither-nor, either-or)*, a list with bullets, and headings in a report.

Example of error: She was interested in doing research on not only the causes of the economic instability in Argentina but also <u>how the Brazilian financial crisis was being solved.</u>

✓ PARALLELISM PRACTICE

Because parallelism can have a great impact on the quality of a document, experienced writers use this technique whenever possible. Parallelism is effective when used in headings of reports, outlines, lists, and within sentences. To practice your skill in detecting errors in parallelism, correct the sentences so that they are in parallel form.

1. The final assignment involves ~~choosing~~ *to choose* a research topic, to read *reading* five sources, and to complete *completing* a ten-page research paper with footnotes and a bibliography. *(or)*

2. Working in a global corporation may be more difficult than to start *starting* your own consulting company.

3. The new position *will* neither presents *present* more challenges than the former job nor will she receive a higher salary.

4. Jane's internship in the Wall Street firm has been effective in increasing her knowledge of stock and bond trading, sharpening her technical skills, and ~~in a great improvement in~~ *greatly improving* her ability to negotiate.

5. Students *who are* unusually well prepared by taking advanced placement courses and ~~who have~~ *having* high SAT scores on the verbal test will be exempted from College Writing at the University of Virginia.

6. The research study will consider the ~~growing~~ number of obese people *that is growing* in the United States, ~~why~~ *that* people are exercising less, and that the portions of food in restaurants ~~have become~~ *are becoming* larger.

7. Alberto will have to take courses in both technical writing and ~~how to design~~ *designing* graphics.

8. The director asked for the following information: the instructor's name, ~~how~~ *the # of* ~~many~~ participants ~~were~~ enrolled, and the location of the workshop.

CONCISE PUNCTUATION REVIEW: PERIOD, ── COMMA, SEMICOLON, COLON, QUOTATION MARKS ──

Read the rules for these punctuation marks, and discuss the examples that follow the rules.

Period Usage

Put a period at the end of a sentence.

Jacob is writing a paper on the French Revolution in 1789. He has always had an interest in that subject because his family is of French origin.

Comma Usage

Separate independent clauses with a comma if they are divided by a conjunction.

Jacob stayed up all night to finish the paper, but he still didn't hand it in on time.

Follow a sentence connector that introduces an independent clause with a comma.

Jacob stayed up all night to finish the paper. Nevertheless, he still didn't hand it in on time.

Separate items in a series with commas.

Erica's paper compared the economies of Brazil, Peru, Argentina, and Colombia. (The comma before *and* in a series is sometimes considered optional. It is never used in newspaper or magazine writing.)

Semicolon Usage

Separate two independent clauses with a semicolon if they are closely related in thought and no conjunction connects them.

Jacob stayed up all night to finish the paper; he still didn't hand it in on time.

Use a semicolon before a sentence connector that connects two independent clauses.

Jacob stayed up all night to finish the paper; however, he still didn't hand it in on time.

Use a semicolon to separate items in a series that have internal punctuation.

During her vacation, Erica traveled to these locations in Latin America: Rio de Janeiro, Brazil; Lima, Peru; Buenos Aires, Argentina; and Bogota, Colombia.

Colon Usage

A colon is used after an independent clause to indicate that the following information is needed to complete the meaning of the sentence.

Erica explained the purpose of the paper: to determine the extent to which economic stability and direct investment were related in Latin American countries.

A colon is used to introduce a formal quotation.

In "Speed" (*The New Yorker,* August 23, 2004), Oliver Sacks states: "As a boy, I was fascinated by speed, the wild range of speeds in the world around me. People moved at different speeds; animals much more so."

Quotation Marks Usage

Double quotation marks are used for direct quotations.

The lecturer said: "Communication is the process of exchanging information among people."

<u>Note:</u> Quotations introduced by *that* are indirect and do not require quotation marks.

The lecturer said that communication is the process of exchanging information among people.

Double quotation marks are placed around words, phrases, and sentences that are copied exactly from a source, such as an article, book, or website. Double quotation marks are also placed around the title of an article in a magazine or journal or a book chapter.

According to Laura D'Andrea Tyson in "For Developing Countries, Health Is Wealth," the poor health of people in developing countries "both reflects their poverty and contributes to it" (20).

CONCISE PUNCTUATION REVIEW:
——— COMMA SPLICE, RUN-ON SENTENCE, FRAGMENT ———

After reviewing the punctuation rules, read the sentences that are not punctuated correctly. Then review the different ways the errors can be corrected.

Comma Splice

A comma splice is two complete sentences (independent clauses) connected with a comma. Do not connect two independent clauses with a comma. Use a period or a semicolon, or a comma followed by a coordinate conjunction. You can also restructure the sentence with an adverbial clause.

Error: **Jacob stayed up all night to finish the paper, he still didn't hand it in on time.**

Jacob stayed up all night to finish the paper. He still didn't hand it in on time.

Jacob stayed up all night to finish the paper; he still didn't hand it in on time.

Jacob stayed up all night to finish the paper, but he still didn't hand it in on time.

Although Jacob stayed up all night to finish the paper, he still didn't hand it in on time.

Run-on Sentence

A run-on sentence is two complete sentences (independent clauses) connected without any punctuation to separate them. Two independent clauses should be separated by a period, a semicolon, or a comma followed by a conjunction. You can also restructure the sentence with an adverbial clause.

Error: **Jacob stayed up all night to finish the paper he still didn't hand it in on time.**

> Jacob stayed up all night to finish the paper. He still didn't hand it in on time.

> Jacob stayed up all night to finish the paper; he still didn't hand it in on time.

> Jacob stayed up all night to finish the paper, but he still didn't hand it in on time.

> Although Jacob stayed up all night to finish the paper, he still didn't hand it in on time.

Fragment

A sentence fragment is a group of words that ends with a period but does not form a complete sentence. A sentence must have a subject, predicate or verb, and complete meaning.

Error: **No independent clause: Because of the extremely negative financial analysis.**

> Because of the extremely negative financial analysis, she didn't invest her money in that fund.

Error: **No predicate: Students that don't own cell phones.**

> Students that don't own cell phones may be at a disadvantage.

Error: **No subject: Is a controversial topic.**

> Capital punishment is a controversial topic.

✓ PUNCTUATION EXERCISE 1: SENTENCE STRUCTURE

Read the statements, and identify each as correct (C), fragment (F), run-on (R), or comma splice (CS). Correct the fragments, run-ons, and comma splices by adding necessary punctuation and/or words. (There are many ways to correct these errors, so discuss the various possibilities when checking your answers in class.)

___F___ 1. The question of whether to hold a formal graduation ceremony.

___R___ 2. Mr. Warren is our new dean of students he does not have a Ph.D.

___F___ 3. The issue under consideration today.

___C___ 4. Although Karl is an expert on bilingual education, he is not on the policy committee.

___F___ 5. To show the exact steps in the procedure.

___CS___ 6. The computer is working fairly well, nevertheless, we are hoping to trade it in for a new one.

___F___ 7. Because his research paper is coming along so slowly.

___C___ 8. While Sandra has much experience in PowerPoint, we don't want her to do the training.

___F___ 9. Although her spoken English is better than mine.

___C___ 10. Her spoken English is better than mine, but I have better listening skills.

___CS___ 11. Their decision was based on extensive analysis, however, I disagree with it.

___CS___ 12. Ms. Gresham is in charge of our computer system, she has a master's degree in information technology.

___R___ 13. Mr. Mendez is our Internet coordinator he also works on advance planning.

___F___ 14. If Lucy has the time and energy.

_____ 15. Since Gloria has the time, she will be able to run the conference.

_____ 16. That report from the director is both comprehensive and persuasive.

_____ 17. Going to make a change in the requirements next semester.

_____ 18. Oscar went to the library to get the videotapes, then he brought the tapes to the classroom.

_____ 19. That clever and sophisticated student from Taiwan.

_____ 20. Hiroko is a reliable and creative student, we need more students like her.

_____ 21. Ms. Donovan, using her laptop computer and talking on her cell phone.

_____ 22. Gieorgio and Claudia are finally having their meeting, in fact, they plan to meet once a week.

_____ 23. Have all the members of the class responded to the survey?

_____ 24. Even though his suggestion has validity.

_____ 25. Having finished the presentation on culture shock, the speaker answered questions from the audience.

✓ PUNCTUATION EXERCISE 2: PARAGRAPH COHERENCE

Some of these statements are correct, but most contain punctuation and sentence structure errors. Correct the errors so that all the sentences together form a logical paragraph. Do not change the order of the sentences, but you should connect several statements and add necessary words. (There are many ways to do this task; no one way is correct.)

1. Being fluent in English is essential today, especially now that English has become the global language. (correct)

2. Is something almost everyone will have to master in the future.
   Its

3. When you can speak English, you have many advantages.

4. For example being able to communicate with other English speakers around the world.

5. Although it is not easy to master English,

6. There are many different methods you can use to learn this language.

7. Including studying in an Intensive English Program, hiring a tutor for private classes, and watching television and movies.

8. An intensive English course is generally the best method, in fact studying in a group is an excellent way to get support and encouragement.

9. Of course motivation is important in studying a foreign language.

10. Because research on language acquisition shows that highly motivated people learn more quickly than those who aren't as motivated.

11. Nevertheless, even if they have strong motivation.

12. Most people need six months to a year to become proficient.

13. Just like many challenges in life.

14. Learning English may be difficult and discouraging at times, so remember that it is well worth the time and effort involved.

✔ PROOFREADING AND EDITING: "MY HEALTHY LIFESTYLE"

Work with a partner to evaluate the rough draft of the short essay "My Healthy Lifestyle." First proofread the essay by identifying errors in grammar and mechanics and correcting them. Using the Proofreader's Checklist, underline the mistakes you find. Then edit the essay's content, style, and organization, using the Editor's Checklist. After you complete the proofreading and editing, discuss your corrections and revisions with your classmates, and compare your revisions with the corrected version of the essay in Appendix G.

PROOFREADER'S CHECKLIST

Grammar

- Do the verbs agree with their subjects?
- Do pronouns agree with their referents?
- Are there any dangling modifiers?
- Are prepositions used correctly?
- Are articles used correctly?
- Are verb tenses used correctly?
- Are parallel structures used when appropriate?

Punctuation

- Are there any comma splices, run-on sentences, or sentence fragments?
- Are periods, commas, semicolons, and colons used correctly?
- Are quotation marks used correctly for direct quotations?

EDITOR'S CHECKLIST

- Does the introduction end with a precise thesis statement?
- Do the body paragraphs support the thesis statement (main idea)?
- Does each body paragraph have a topic sentence related to the thesis?
- Do the remaining sentences in each paragraph support the topic sentence?
- Are facts, statistics, examples, or quotations used to expand on the topic sentence?
- Are the paragraphs unified, coherent, and appropriate in length?
- Do sentence connectors (transition words) add coherence to the paragraphs?
- Are the verbs, adjectives, and adverbs used effectively?
- Is the conclusion meaningful and logical?
- Is the style of the document clear and concise, without redundancy?

My Healthy Lifestyle

Since I have been in Washington, DC, my lifestyle has been generally healthy in regards to my diet but I exercise more in Colombia compared to here. Actually, I try to keep myself healthy everyday. Fortunately, there are many excellent inexpensive restaurants and many sightseeing places and museum where I can walk around in Washington, DC. It's nice opportunity to eat anything and to exercise. And I remember not to eat too much fat and sugar whenever I eat. Of course sometimes is difficult to do, especially since fast food restaurant as McDonalds are everywhere I look. Living in Washington, DC is different than life in Colombia in many ways.

After I came to the United States, it is true that my eating habit has changed. I no longer eat Latin American food that is my favorite food that I eat everyday in Colombia. Really I am missing the fresh fruits and vegetables of my country. But, I can eat anything and I am flexible and curious about any food. I enjoy eating very much. In the United States, I can choose any kinds of food everywhere, because there are many foodstuffs. Thus I thinking about what is good for my health. I guess is important to think about what is needed to my health and pay attention for nutrition, no matter where I am. If I can do it, I must keep myself healthy while staying here.

On the other hand, it is difficult for me to exercise. Because I don't like the cold weather and in fact, I don't have as much time to exercise as in Colombia. But since I like walking, I walk between the Rosslyn metro station and the university sometimes. Although this is only a small thing, I think is more helpful for my health to do something than do nothing. In addition, I go to walk around Washington on the weekend, which is a beautiful city, taking care about my health and getting the exercise. For example last weekend I have walked from the Lincoln Memorial to the Washington Monument.

I really enjoy my life in Washington, DC, and I adjusted to this new culture real well. And I would like to take advantage from the rest of my stay here, therefore, I plan to keep myself healthy until I come back to Colombia. No matter where I am living, thinking about diet and nutrition by myself are important, exercise should also be a priority.

CHAPTER **5**

Effective Style

Style is the way in which we express ourselves in words. Just as each individual has a unique manner of speaking, so each of us has a unique manner of writing: our writing voice. This style, which includes our tone, can and should be adjusted to suit the needs of a particular assignment. For example, a memorandum in the workplace requires a style and tone that differ from the style and tone of a college essay. The purpose of this chapter is to explain characteristics of an effective style and give guidelines for writing in the academic style used in the United States.

The best writers are in control of their writing style, and they adjust their style in each assignment so that it is appropriate to their purpose and audience. But what exactly does the phrase *writing style* mean, and how can we control it? Although some people think that writing style is an abstract concept, in fact it is a concrete result of the word choice, sentence structure, and paragraph development that we employ to get our message across to our reader. When writing academic documents, we can choose a subjective or objective, formal or informal, technical or non-technical style. (See Appendix B: Examples of Writing Styles.) Our tone can be personal or impersonal, factual or scholarly, humorous or serious, balanced or persuasive, authoritative or tentative. Again, this depends on an analysis of our audience and purpose, which in turn determines our word choice, sentence structure, and paragraph development.

Excellent academic writing is characterized by clarity, coherence, conciseness, and precision. The examples that follow show how to revise writing so that it is clear, coherent, concise, and precise. Rather than constructing simple sentences, try to **combine your ideas** into complex or compound sentences; moreover, **include sentence connectors** to add coherence to your writing. Also, **avoid redundancy,** the unnecessary words that weaken the impact of writing. Finally, don't write in generalities; **write with specificity.** If you follow these suggestions, your writing will have the rare quality of energy, which means that readers will become involved in your ideas and want to continue reading. Without energy, even well-written documents may put most readers to sleep.

—— **PRINCIPLES OF STYLE** ——

Clarity

➡ **Clarity: Expressing meaning with sentence combining**

Original: I have been in Washington, DC, for several months. My lifestyle has been healthy in regard to my diet and exercise. Actually, I try to maintain my health every day. Fortunately, there are many excellent but not too expensive restaurants. There are also many sightseeing places and museums to walk around in Washington, DC. It's a nice opportunity to eat anything and to exercise. And I remember not to eat foods with too much fat and sugar whenever I eat at a restaurant. In Colombia I ate nutritious food every day. (91 words, 8 sentences)

Revision: Since I have been in Washington, DC, my lifestyle has been healthy in regard to my diet and exercise because I pay attention to my health. One way to stay healthy is to exercise by walking, which is easy to do in Washington, with its museums and tourist sites. In addition, Washington has excellent inexpensive restaurants, where I can eat nutritious food like the food I ate in Colombia. (69 words, 3 sentences)

Coherence

➡ **Coherence: Developing ideas in logical, linear order, using sentence connectors**

Original: The assignment involves writing a report that has charts and graphs that show the results of 25 interviews. This report will be based on asking people questions about current issues that are in the news today. Students will have to ask 25 people what they think about these current issues and write up the results of the questionnaire in a report. The interviews will be tape-recorded. (67 words, 4 sentences)

Revision: First, students have to choose a current issue in the news and create a questionnaire about the issue. **Next,** they tape-record interviews with 25 people. **Last,** they write a report on the results of the interviews, including charts and graphs. (41 words, 3 sentences)

Conciseness

➡ **Conciseness: Avoiding redundancy by expressing ideas directly, with few words**

Original: Due to the fact that all the students were thinking about the assignment from their own different points of view, they were not able to reach a group consensus on what they were supposed to accomplish in the assigned task. (40 words)

Revision: Because the students had different viewpoints on the assignment, they couldn't reach a consensus on their goal. (17 words)

Precision

➡ **Precision: Choosing the exact words to convey the intended meaning**

Original: There was a manager's meeting today, and a lot of decisions were made about our new project at the meeting. (20 words)

Revision: The managers decided on the project goals, deadlines, and assignments at today's meeting. (13 words)

───────────────── **STRATEGIES** ─────────────────

Sentence Combining

Combine each group of sentences into one sentence by changing the simple sentences into complex and compound sentences, deleting redundant words, and using parallelism. You can also add sentence connectors. (See Appendix E for a list of sentence connectors, their meaning, and punctuation rules.) The revised sentences should form one complete paragraph. The example contains the topic sentence of the paragraph.

Example: Leda, my roommate, and I don't get along well. We are incompatible. Our personalities clash. We have opposite styles of communication.

Revision: Because my roommate Leda and I have opposite styles of communication and clashing personalities, we are incompatible.

1. Leda was raised in Lima, Peru. She speaks English fluently. We can't communicate with each other.

2. Leda is shy and quiet. I'm an extrovert. I like to express my feelings and beliefs.

3. I come from a big family of four children. I am used to sharing and compromising. Leda is an only child and is somewhat selfish. She probably doesn't realize it.

4. We have opposite body rhythms. She enjoys going to bed late and sleeping until noon. I prefer to go to bed by midnight and get up really early in the morning.

5. Our interests are different. My favorite sport is volleyball, and I am an expert volleyball player. Leda likes to go hiking in the mountains and go swimming in the ocean.

6. I eat anything, even ice cream and fast food, and don't worry about gaining weight. Leda is always on a diet and only eats healthy foods. This is a good example of our lack of compatibility.

7. These problems involve basic lifestyle choices. They also involve styles of communication. All of them do to some degree.

8. This is a serious problem for us. Counseling is one solution to the problem. It may only make the situation worse. We may say things to each other that we will regret.

9. There is another solution. Moving is also an option. One of us could move to a different room in the dorm. I could move into an off-campus apartment. An apartment could be expensive.

10. Of course, we should attempt to work out our problems. Once we do, we will be much happier. We will be able to concentrate on our studies. We will be able to enjoy our college life.

Paragraph Coherence: "Making Copies"

The paragraphs that follow lack coherence because they are written in short, choppy sentences, without sentence connectors or conjunctions. After reading the paragraphs, revise them by combining some of the sentences, deleting redundant words, and adding sentence connectors. These paragraphs are based on "Making Copies" by David Owen, published in *Smithsonian* magazine and in the book *Copies in Seconds* (Simon & Schuster, 2004).[1] This article describes the man who invented the copy machine, Chester Carlson.

Copying is the engine of civilization: culture is behavior duplicated. The oldest copier invented by people is language. Language makes an idea of yours become an idea of mine. The second great copying machine was writing. The Sumerians transposed spoken words into stylus marks on clay tablets. They did that more than 5,000 years ago. They hugely extended the human network. Language had created the human network. Writing freed copying from the chain of living contact. It made ideas permanent. It made them portable. It made them endlessly reproducible. (89 words, 12 sentences)

Johann Gutenberg invented the printing press. He did that in the mid-1400s. Before he invented the printing press, producing a book in an edition of more than one generally meant writing it out again. Printing with moveable type was not copying. Gutenberg couldn't take a document and feed it into his printing press and run off facsimiles. This document already existed. The first true mechanical copier was manufactured in 1780. At that time,

[1] David Owen, "Making Copies," *Smithsonian*, August 2004, 91–92.

James Watt created the copying press. James Watt is better known as the inventor of the modern steam engine. Few people today know what a copying press was. You may have seen one in an antiques store. It was perhaps called a book press. (117 words, 12 sentences)

Copying presses were standard equipment in offices for nearly a century and a half. (Thomas Jefferson used one. Calvin Coolidge used one. He was the last president whose official correspondence was copied on one.) The machines were displaced. This began to happen in the late 1800s. They were displaced by a combination of two 19th century inventions. They were displaced by the typewriter and carbon paper. (66 words, 8 sentences)

Tone: Word Choice

The writer's tone is another major factor in creating an effective style. Tone refers to the writer's attitude to the subject and to the audience and is revealed primarily through word choice. The tone of a document should remain consistent throughout the document.

A writer's tone may be personal or impersonal, serious or humorous, ironic or satirical, balanced or persuasive, authoritative or tentative, depending on the purpose of the document and the audience. Most academic documents, especially those that involve research, require an impersonal, balanced, and factual tone.

ANALYSIS OF TONE: *RIVER OUT OF EDEN*

Richard Dawkins is a British scientist who wrote *River Out of Eden: A Darwinian View of Life*. This book about Charles Darwin's theory of evolution explains complex ideas in a simple way. In 1859 Charles Darwin published *On the Origin of Species,* in which he presented his theory of evolution, natural selection. According to this theory, life forms change through time, and environmental conditions (nature) determine the survival and reproduction of an organism. Organisms with more adaptive traits will live, and those with less adaptive traits will die out. While Darwin's theory of evolution is generally accepted today, there are those who do not agree with it. After you read the excerpt from *River Out of Eden,* discuss the author's ideas, and answer the questions that follow.

Chapter 1: The Digital River[2]

All peoples have epic legends about their tribal ancestors, and these legends often formalize themselves into religious cults. People revere and even worship their ancestors—as well they might, for it is real ancestors, not supernatural gods, that hold the key to understanding life. Of all organisms born, the majority die before they come of age. Of the minority that survive and breed, an even smaller minority will have a descendant alive a thousand generations hence. This tiny minority of a minority, this progenitorial elite, is all that future generations will be able to call ancestral. Ancestors are rare, [but] descendants are common.

All organisms that have ever lived—every animal and plant, all bacteria and all fungi, every creeping thing, and all readers of this book—can look back at their ancestors and make the following proud claim: Not a single one of

[2] Richard Dawkins, *River Out of Eden: A Darwinian View of Life* (New York: HarperCollins, Inc., 1995), 1–2.

our ancestors died in infancy. They all reached adulthood, and every single one was capable of finding at least one heterosexual partner and of successfully copulating. Not a single one of our ancestors was felled by an enemy, or by a virus, or by a misjudged footstep on a cliff edge, before bringing at least one child into the world. Thousands of our ancestors' contemporaries failed in all these respects, but not a single solitary one of our ancestors failed in any of them. These statements are blindingly obvious, yet from them much follows: much that is curious and unexpected, much that explains and much that astonishes. All these matters will be the subject of this book.

- What is the purpose of this excerpt?
- Who is the intended audience for this book?
- How does the author support his main idea?
- What pronouns are used in this excerpt?
- What adjectives and adverbs are used?
- Is the tone of this paragraph personal or impersonal?

✔ WORD CHOICE: OBJECTIVITY

Rewrite the sentences to give them an objective and factual tone that would be appropriate to a research essay or report.

1. Because of the incredible decrease in the inflation rate, I hope the economic problems in Italy will settle down sooner or later.

2. In my personal opinion, we naive consumers should not buy products made by evil companies that use child labor.

3. You will have no problem accepting our accurate conclusion after you finish reading our superior report.

4. I really wish I could have interviewed more than 25 people so that I could be sure I was on the right track in reporting the results of our survey, but I did the best I could.

5. The only way to get a handle on the situation was to hang out with the big execs and get the real story on what went wrong with their accounting procedures.

6. The journalist wrote an outstanding article in the *New York Times* that revealed the whole truth about the president's brilliant foreign policy.

7. Your approach to reorganization is old-fashioned and will never lead to getting rid of the lazy workers.

8. It seems to me that if you blame the increase in outsourcing for the high unemployment rate in the United States, you are making a bad mistake.

✔ **ANALYSIS OF TONE: "GENDER EQUALITY IN CHINA"**

Read the short report "Gender Equality in China" and analyze the tone by considering the writer's choice of pronouns, adjectives, and adverbs. Then circle the words on this list that best describe the tone of the essay.

personal	balanced	humorous	factual	authoritative
impersonal	persuasive	serious	literary	tentative

CHAPTER 5: Effective Style · **61**

Gender Equality in China

China, whose formal name is the People's Republic of China, grants women the same rights in political, economic, cultural, social and family life as men have. Thus, in China, which has a communist government, women have achieved gender equality to some degree.

As for voting, Chinese women enjoy the same rights as men to vote and to stand for election. The National People's Congress and all levels of the local People's Congress have to have adequate numbers of women deputies and are working to gradually increase the number of women deputies.

The property rights of women are equal to those of men and are protected by the state. Women's legal rights to common property in marriage are guaranteed. These rights are protected after women get divorced. For instance, at the time of divorce, husbands and wives shall divide their jointly owned house in accordance with their agreement. If they fail to reach an agreement, the People's Court shall pass judgment in accordance with the principle of giving favorable consideration to the rights of women and children. The equal property inheritance right enjoyed by women is also protected by law.

Husbands and wives of child-bearing age must practice family planning, and with exceptions, a family is allowed to have only one child. The health departments have to protect the health and safety of women using birth control or having birth control surgery to meet family planning requirements.

Generally speaking, after a divorce, wives leave their houses, and husbands are awarded guardianship over the children. If a father can't serve as the guardian of his children for some reason, no one shall interfere with the mother's guardianship. At the time of divorce, in dealing with the question of rearing children, favorable consideration has to be given to the wife's reasonable demands and to the rights and interests of the children if she has lost child-bearing ability because of sterilization or other reasons.

Although women in China are nearly equal to men from the standpoint of legal rights, at the time of divorce, wives are at a disadvantage to husbands in gaining custody of the children. Consequently, women in China even now have room to improve their conditions with regard to gender equality.

Works Cited

"Law Safeguarding Women's Rights and Interests of the People's Republic of China." Chinalaw Web. The University of Maryland. 2000. <http://www.qis.net/chinalaw/>.

RESEARCH REPORT

Do Internet research to find information on women's human and civil rights in various countries. (Suggested websites are listed.) Choose one country and investigate whether women have the following rights: voting, serving in parliament or congress, running for elective office, owning property, having an abortion, getting a divorce, gaining custody of children in case of divorce, inheriting money or property, and serving in the military.

Write a short report based on the information you have collected. The tone of the report should be impersonal, balanced, and factual. You can develop your own thesis, or you may prefer to use this one: *In* _____, *women have achieved/have not achieved gender equality.*

List your sources at the end of the report as Works Cited. Alphabetize the sources according to the last name of the author. If no author is identified, list the sources by the first word of the title, not including *a, an,* or *the.*

Suggested Websites

- The Association for Women's Rights in Development: *www.awid.org/*
- Human Rights Watch: *www.hrw.org/*
- International Center for Research on Women: *www.icrw.org/*
- Madre: *www.madre.org/*
- United Nations Development Fund for Women: *www.unifem.org/*
- The United Nations: *www.un.org/*
- Women in Development NET Work: *www.focusintl.com/widnet.htm*
- The World Bank Group: *www.worldbank.org/* (Click Data & Statistics. Under Popular Resources, click GenderStats.)

✓ ANALYSIS OF STYLE: "MAKING COPIES"

Read the excerpt taken from "Making Copies" on pages 64–65, an article by David Owen in *Smithsonian* magazine about the man who invented the copy machine, Chester Carlson. Identify the techniques that contribute to the clarity, coherence, conciseness, and precision of Owen's style, and also note its energetic quality. Underline the examples in the text that support your analysis.

- Sentence combining
- Sentence connectors
- Interesting adjectives and adverbs
- Strong, active verbs
- Variety of sentence structure
- Relevant quotations
- Consistency of tone

Making Copies[3]

DAVID OWEN

Remarkably, xerography was conceived by one person—Chester Carlson, a shy, soft-spoken patent attorney, who grew up in almost unspeakable poverty and worked his way through junior college and the California Institute or Technology. He made his discovery in solitude in 1937 and offered it to more than 20 major corporations, among them IBM, General Electric, Eastman Kodak and RCA. All of them turned him down, expressing what he later called "an enthusiastic lack of interest" and thereby passing up the opportunity to manufacture what *Fortune* magazine would describe as "the most successful product ever marketed in America."

Carlson's invention was indeed a commercial triumph. Essentially overnight, people began making copies at a rate that was orders of magnitude higher than anyone had believed possible. And the rate is still growing. In fact, most documents handled by a typical American office worker today are produced xerographically, either on copiers manufactured by Xerox and its competitors or on laser printers, which employ the same process (and were invented in the 1970s, by a Xerox researcher). This year, the world will produce more than three trillion xerographic copies and laser-printed pages—about 500 for every human on earth.

Xerography eventually made Carlson a very wealthy man. (His royalties amounted to something like a 16th of a cent for every Xerox copy made, worldwide, through 1965.) Nevertheless, he lived simply. He never owned a second home or a second car, and his wife had to urge him not to buy third-class train tickets when he traveled in Europe. People who knew him casually seldom suspected

[3] Owen, "Making Copies," 92.

that he was rich or even well-to-do; when Carlson told an acquaintance he worked at Xerox, the man assumed he was a factory worker and asked if he belonged to a union. "His real wealth seemed to be composed of the number of things he could easily do without," his second wife said. He spent the last years of his life quietly giving most of his fortune away. When he died in 1968, among the eulogizers was the secretary-general of the United Nations.

 **ASSIGNMENT**   Research Report

Do Internet research on a person who invented or discovered something of major importance to society. Then write a short report about this person and his or her invention or discovery. The tone of this report should be impersonal, balanced, and factual. Cite the sources of your information using the MLA in-text citation style, and list the sources at the end of the report as Works Cited. Alphabetize the sources according the last name of the author. If no author is identified, list the sources by the first word of the title, not including *a*, *an*, or *the*.

CHAPTER

The Cohesive Paragraph

STRATEGIES

The paragraph is the building block of longer documents, and it takes precision and control to write an excellent paragraph. In fact, it can be more challenging to write a good paragraph than to write an entire essay. A cohesive paragraph is logically developed, well structured, and complete as a unit of meaning. It is characterized by unity and coherence and contains an effective topic sentence, supporting sentences, and a concluding sentence.

Unity

A good paragraph is cohesive because the sentences are interconnected. It discusses one topic in a unified way, including only relevant statements that support the main idea. Ideas that are irrelevant should be deleted.

Coherence

The sentences in a paragraph are logically organized so that each sentence flows naturally from the one before and leads naturally to the one following in an organic development of ideas.

Topic Sentence

A paragraph requires a clear topic sentence that presents the main idea or purpose of that paragraph to the reader. While this sentence should be broad enough to cover all the information in the paragraph, it should also contain a controlling idea, which may be a key word or phrase. This topic sentence is usually the first sentence in the paragraph, but it can be placed at the end, functioning as both a topic and a concluding sentence. A paragraph can also begin with two topic sentences that express related ideas.

> **Example of a topic sentence:** Immigrants who come to the United States will benefit greatly from learning the English language; however, many states do not offer enough educational resources.

Supporting Sentences

The remainder of the paragraph contains supporting sentences with specific facts, statistics, examples, or quotations. These sentences flow logically from the opening (topic) sentence and help to create the qualities of unity and coherence that characterize effective paragraphs.

Concluding Sentence

The last sentence of a paragraph sometimes presents a concluding statement that refers back to the topic sentence or paraphrases the topic sentence. Alternatively, in a multi-paragraph essay, the last sentence may serve as a bridge or transition sentence that leads to the following paragraph.

Length

The length of a paragraph is critical to its effectiveness. In general, paragraphs should not be longer than 200 words or shorter than 50 words. Readers sometimes have difficulty processing paragraphs that are more than 200 words. If necessary, divide an extremely long paragraph into two sections, each with its own topic sentence.

The following is an example of a well-crafted paragraph on the topic of providing English language education for immigrants (121 words).

English Language Education

Topic Sentence: Immigrants who come to the United States will benefit greatly from learning the English language; however, many states do not offer enough educational resources.

Supporting Sentences: In Montgomery County, Maryland, a county with a large number of non-native speakers of English, "105,000 residents have 'limited English' skills, yet the classes for adults who want to learn can accommodate only about 24,000 people," according to council-member Tom Perez. In fact, in 2003, the English classes had a waiting list of 2,000 adults.[1] This lack of resources must be remedied by the state and county governments.

Concluding Sentence: They should provide the necessary funding for English language courses so that immigrants will not be disadvantaged as they struggle to learn about and adapt to American culture.

---

[1] Darragh Johnson and Matthew Mosk, "Immigrant Remark Still Burns," *Washington Post*, May 15, 2004, B1.

--- **EVALUATION AND EDITING** ---

Read the paragraphs and evaluate them in terms of their unity, coherence, topic sentences, supporting sentences, concluding sentences, and length. After discussing the paragraphs with a partner, edit them so that they are unified and coherent.

Teaching English

Teaching English as a Second Language has become an important profession in the United States in the twenty-first century, and the number of college graduates entering this field is growing rapidly. Many adult immigrants who need to acquire proficiency in English are searching for affordable schools. They realize that being able to communicate well in English is a valuable and necessary skill in terms of adjusting to American society, assimilating into the culture, and finding a job. Of course, some immigrants continue to use their native languages, but their children learn English in school and become bilingual, which is a great advantage. One question that remains unanswered today is whether English should be the official language of the United States. This question has been debated for many years. Americans have strong opinions on the subject, and both sides have valid arguments. However, it is unlikely that the U.S. Congress will pass an amendment to the Constitution making English the official language. Rather, English will be the dominant language, but people will be free to communicate in whatever language they prefer.

Paragraph Evaluation

Excellent +	Satisfactory √	Unsatisfactory –
• Unity		_____
• Coherence		_____
• Topic Sentence		_____
• Supporting Sentences		_____
• Concluding Sentence		_____
• Length		_____

College Costs

The cost of a college education in the United States is growing every year at twice the inflation rate, and it is now about double what it was in the 1980s. Costs at public colleges increased by 13 percent in 2002, and they rose 47 percent over the past decade.[2] They also rose at private universities, but at a slower rate. Today, including room and board, "the average student now pays $26,854 a year to attend a private university, and $10,636 to attend a public university in his or her own state."[3] And that does not cover books, laptop computers, or clothes. This means it could cost nearly $50,000 for an in-state resident to attend the University of Virginia for four years.[4] Parents are worried that they will not be able to afford to send their children to col-

---

[2] Michael Dobbs, "Tuition Soars at Public Colleges," *Washington Post*, October 22, 2003, A03.

[3] Ibid.

[4] Albert B. Crenshaw, "Higher Education Is Still Affordable, with Planning," *Washington Post*, October 5, 2003, F04.

lege, and many are investing their money in special college funds, beginning at the time of their child's birth. In the 1990's, tuition at the finest private universities was about $15,000 annually, and at public colleges it was about $5,000. One positive result of this increase in college costs has been a corresponding increase in financial aid, with student aid rising "to a record $105 billion."[5] Almost all universities and colleges offer this aid to admitted students, depending upon the financial need of the students. In fact, Harvard has implemented a policy that waives all college expenses of students whose families make under $40,000 a year.[6] Moreover, many educational institutions provide full scholarships to deserving students who excel in certain areas such as academics or athletics. There are also government loans, such as Pell Grants, for college education. According to the American Council of Education, students who receive grants and loans pay about $1,700 yearly to attend a public college.[7] Perhaps this explains why, despite the extremely high cost of higher education, more students are enrolling in colleges and universities than ever before.

[5] Dobbs, "Tuition Soars at Public Colleges," A03.
[6] Jay Mathews, "Invitation to Disappointment," *Washington Post*, June 5, 2004, A22.
[7] Dobbs, "Tuition Soars at Public Colleges," A03.

Paragraph Evaluation

Excellent +	Satisfactory √	Unsatisfactory –
• Unity		_____
• Coherence		_____
• Topic Sentence		_____
• Supporting Sentences		_____
• Concluding Sentence		_____
• Length		_____

ANALYSIS: *THE BLIND WATCHMAKER*

Read the paragraph from *The Blind Watchmaker* by the British scientist Richard Dawkins. Dawkins, who is a professor at Oxford University in England, writes about Charles Darwin's theory of evolution, natural selection, and other evolution theories. Identify the components of the paragraph by labeling them in the margin: topic sentence, supporting sentences, concluding sentence.

The Blind Watchmaker[8]
Chapter 9: Puncturing Punctuationism[9]

Darwin's answer to the question of the origin of the species was, in a general sense, that species were descended from other species. Moreover, the family tree of life is a branching one, which means that more than one modern species can be traced back to one ancestral one. For instance, lions and tigers are now members of different species, but they have both sprung from a single ancestral species, probably not very long ago. This ancestral species may have been the same as one of the two modern species; or it may have been a third modern species; or maybe it is now extinct. Similarly, humans and chimps now clearly belong to different species, but their ancestors of a few million years ago belonged to one single species. Speciation is the process by which a single species becomes two species, one of which may be the same as the original single one.

---

[8] Richard Darwin, *The Blind Watchmaker: Why the Evidence of Evolution Reveals a Universe without Design* (New York: W. W. Norton & Company, 1996), 236–37.

[9] *Punctuationism* is a theory of evolution. According to this theory, evolution was not a smooth sequence of gradual change but occurred in sudden bursts. *Puncturing* means deflating or destroying.

ASSIGNMENT Extended Definition—The Meaning of Freedom

Words have both **denotations** (dictionary definitions) and **connotations** (meanings beyond the dictionary, such as emotional and psychological meanings). A good example of a word with a variety of connotations is the word *freedom. Merriam-Webster's Collegiate Dictionary* provides at least ten definitions, but this word has a unique meaning to each individual. Read this definition of freedom, which is from *Merriam-Webster's*.

1. the quality or state of being free; as
   a: the absence of necessity, coercion, or constraint in choice of action
   b: liberation from slavery or restraint or from the power of another; independence

Write one paragraph about the meaning of the word *freedom*. This paragraph should include a dictionary definition and the particular meaning that this word has to you. While you are writing, pay attention to the characteristics of an excellent paragraph: unity and coherence. When you have completed the first draft of this paragraph, edit it by answering these questions. Then share it with your classmates.

- Does your paragraph discuss only one point?
- Are the ideas developed logically?
- Does the topic sentence present the main idea of your paragraph clearly? Is it broad enough to cover all the information in the paragraph but also focused on a controlling idea?
- Is the paragraph cohesive? Do the remaining sentences support and expand upon the topic sentence?
- Are there specific facts, statistics, examples, or quotations?
- Is there a concluding sentence?
- Is the paragraph about 200 words long?

The Meaning of Freedom

_____

_____

_____

_____

_____

_____

_____

_____

_____

_____

ASSIGNMENT   Response Writing

What is your opinion on how the world was created? Do you believe in Charles Darwin's theory of evolution? In 1859 Darwin published _On the Origin of Species_, a book that presented his theory of evolution, natural selection. According to this theory, life forms change through time, and environmental conditions (nature) determine the survival and reproduction of an organism. Organisms with more adaptive traits will live, and those with less adaptive traits will die out. While Darwin's theory of evolution is generally accepted today, there are those who do not agree with it.

This excerpt is from Richard Dawkins's _River Out of Eden: A Darwinian View of Life_. Dawkins writes books about Charles Darwin's theory of evolution and explains these complex ideas in a simple way. After thinking about Dawkins's explanation of why some people do not accept Darwin's theory of evolution, write a one- or two-paragraph response. When you have completed this response, share it with your classmates by reading it aloud.

Note: If you are interested in learning more about Charles Darwin, you can access this website: BBC Education: Evolution Website: Charles Darwin at _www.bbc.co.uk/education/darwin/_. This site contains a wealth of information on Darwin, including an article by Richard Dawkins titled "Darwin and Darwinism."

Chapter 9: Puncturing Punctuationism[10]

There are people in the world who desperately want not to have to believe in Darwinism. They seem to fall into three main classes. First, there are those who, for religious reasons, want evolution itself to be untrue. Second, there are those who have no reason to deny that evolution has happened but who, often for political or ideological reasons, find Darwin's theory of its *mechanism* distasteful. Of these, some find the idea of natural selection unacceptably harsh and ruthless; others confuse natural selection with randomness, and hence 'meaninglessness', which offends their dignity; yet others confuse Darwinism with Social Darwinism, which has racist and other disagreeable overtones. Third, there are people, including many working in what they call (often as a singular noun) 'the media', who just like seeing applecarts upset, perhaps because it makes good journalistic copy, and Darwinism has become sufficiently established and respectable to be a tempting applecart.

<u>Note:</u> Richard Dawkins, a professor at Oxford University in England, uses the British style of punctuation, which differs from the American punctuation style. This style uses single, rather than double, quotation marks around a word and places the comma outside, rather than inside, the quotation marks. In this paragraph, Dawkins includes an idiom, *to upset the applecart,* which means to rebel against an accepted belief or system. See footnote on page 73 for an explanation of punctuationism.

[10] Darwin, *The Blind Watchmaker,* 250–51.

The Accurate Summary

PREVIEW

➤ **Active Reading**

➤ **Critical Analysis**

➤ **Verb Tense**

➤ **Paraphrasing**

A **summary** is a brief restatement of a longer written document. Its purpose is to convey knowledge in a clear and concise form, so the summarizer must extract only the most important information from the entire document. Writing accurate summaries is challenging because it depends on the skills of reading comprehension, critical analysis, and paraphrasing. Summaries can be as short as one sentence or as long as several pages, but generally they are about one-third to one-fourth the length of the original document.

Writers do not give their opinions in a summary unless the assignment specifically asks for a summary and response to the ideas in the article or book, in which case the assignment would be a reaction paper. The summarizer is restricted to including <u>only</u> the information in the original document, without adding additional ideas, drawing inferences, or making personal comments. In other words, the writer reports objectively on the content of an article or book. In reality, however, a writer may use a verb or adverb that reveals a bias. For example, "Paul Gray *claims* that" has a negative tone compared to "Paul Gray *says* that." And "Doris Kearns Goodwin *convincingly* justifies her citation errors" differs from "Doris Kearns Goodwin *attempts to justify* her citation errors." Keep in mind the power of each word as you select your verbs and adverbs.

In the academic world, students are often required to write summaries of books, chapters in books, articles, or lectures. Students may also write summaries as a study strategy to confirm understanding of a passage or a lecture and to prepare for a test. (Summarizing is now tested on high-stakes tests like the TOEFL®.) In the working world, summary writing is a skill that is in great demand because managers can save time by reading summaries rather than entire documents. Learning to separate the essential from the nonessential information takes concentration and effort, but writers can do so through active reading and critical analysis.

STRATEGIES

Active Reading: Preview, Read, Review

In order to summarize a document, you must have a high level of comprehension of its meaning, including difficult vocabulary words, as well as an understanding of the author's unique style and possibly subtle shadings of tone. You must be able to read between the lines—to see that there may be more than just what is literally said. Being an active reader by interacting with the text and responding to the author's ideas will improve your reading comprehension.

In preparation for summarizing, you can strengthen your reading skills by reading an article or book at least three times. The first time is your **preview** of the reading, a quick look at the author, title, first and last paragraphs, and topic sentences. The second time you should read the book or article carefully, with a pen, pencil, or highlighter in your hand. Become an active participant in the reading process by annotating (making comments on) the reading and underlining topic sentences, key terms/vocabulary, and supporting data. During the third reading, you should **review** what you underlined and continue annotating by circling new vocabulary words and highlighting any phrases or sentences that you cannot understand so that you can return to the passage later.

Critical Analysis

Writing an effective summary demands the ability to think analytically about the document you are summarizing in order to identify the main idea, major points, and the supporting facts and statistics. You must be able to extract only the most important information from the original document, omitting minor points and examples. In addition, the summarizer should include the author's tone; for example, if the author has a humorous or ironic tone, that should be part of the summary.

✓ **ANNOTATION TASK: READING ACTIVELY AND ANALYTICALLY**

The excerpt on pages 80–81 is taken from *The Naked Olympics,* a book by Tony Perrottet, who visited the Stadium where the Olympics were held in ancient Greece. While you are reading the paragraphs, annotate them by underlining major points and key terms, circling unfamiliar words and metaphoric language,[1] and making comments in the margin responding to the ideas in the text. When you have completed your reading, compare your annotations with those of a classmate and discuss the differences and similarities. Then write two sentences that summarize the excerpt.

[1] Metaphoric language contains figures of speech (metaphors, similes, personifications) that compare two unlike ideas or objects. (See Appendix A: Definitions of Writing Terms.)

The Naked Olympics[2]

In the hills above Olympia, I awoke with a start before dawn, feeling bleary-eyed from the Greek wine I'd drunk with some rowdy archaeologists the night before. It was going to be a perfect summer's day; from my hotel window I saw clear sky over the mountains of Arcadia, whose peaks covered the horizon like the waves of a wild blue sea. I needed some exercise—a jog to clear my head. But where should I run in this corner of the rural Peloponnese? Where else, it occurred to me, but in the ancient Olympic Stadium?

I arrived at the ruins just before the sun, wearing an old pair of Nikes (named after the winged goddess of Victory). . . . I followed a trail past the fallen columns of great temples, splayed out in the grass like skeletal fingers; purple wildflowers pushed up between memorials to forgotten sports champions. Olympia's idyllic pastoral setting has changed little in the last 2,500 years: the river Alpheus still gurgles in its shady bed alongside the Gymnasium; to the north rises an evenly conical hill, bristling with pine forest, where Zeus had wrestled his father, the Titan Kronos, for control of the world.

Soon a stone archway announced the entrance to the Stadium. . . . Rising on each side of me were earth embankments, now swathed in succulent green lawn. And there, at the very center of the Stadium, was the running

---

[2] Tony Perrottet, *The Naked Olympics: The True Story of the Ancient Games* (New York: Random House, 2004), 3–5.

track—a rectangular expanse of clay, bordered by stone gutters, vaguely suggesting a small landing strip. According to a legend, the track's 210-yard length had been marked out by Hercules himself. For nearly 12 centuries, it was the focus of the greatest recurring festival in Western history.

I approached the ancient starting line—a white marble sill that is miraculously intact—kicked off the Nikes, and instead curled my toes into the premade grooves. Nothing broke the silence except the buzzing of bees in the distance. And then I was off, racing in the footsteps of ancient champions.

✓ CRITICAL ANALYSIS TASK: SUMMARY

The excerpt that begins on page 82 is also taken from *The Naked Olympics* by Tony Perrottet. After reading the paragraphs, identify the main idea and major points. Then write a 50-word summary of the excerpt, paraphrasing the sentences from the original document and placing the main idea at the beginning. You may include a quoted word or phrase if you choose. Share your summary with the class by reading it aloud.

Main Idea

_____

_____

_____

Major Points

_____

_____

_____

_____

_____

Summary

_____

_____

_____

_____

_____

_____

The Naked Olympics[3]

The Games were sensationally popular, the greatest recurring event in antiquity, held without fail every four years from 776 B.C. until the Christian emperors banned pagan festivals in A.D. 394—a mind-boggling run of nearly 1,200 years. For the Greeks, it was considered a great misfortune to die without having been to Olympia. One Athenian baker boasted on his gravestone that he had attended the Games 12 times. "By heaven!" raved the holy man Apollonius of Tyana, "Nothing in the world of men is so agreeable or dear to the Gods."

. . . What kept the hordes [fans] coming back, generation after generation? It was a question that the Athenian philosopher and sports buff Epictetus pondered late in the first century. He argued that the Olympics were a metaphor for human existence itself. Every day was filled with difficulties and tribulations: unbearable heat, pushy crowds, grime, noise, and endless petty annoyances. "But of course you put up with it all," he said, "because it's an unforgettable spectacle." . . .

[3] Ibid., 9–11.

> Sports were only one part of the festival. The Games were actually the ultimate pagan entertainment package, where every human diversion would be found at once, on and off the field. Each Olympiad was an expression of Hellenic unity, an all-consuming pageant, . . . as spiritually profound for pagans as a pilgrimage to Varanasi for Hindus or Mecca for Muslims.) The site had grand procession routes, dozens of altars, public banquet halls, booths for sideshow artists.

Verb Tense

A summary should be written in the present tense, but many summary writers shift from one verb tense to another, which creates a confusing and disjointed tone. Choosing the correct tenses when writing a summary is not easy because the document that is being summarized probably contains a variety of verb tenses. Nevertheless, when you are discussing and summarizing an author's ideas, whether from works of literature or articles in journals, newspapers, or websites, the academic convention requires that you use the present tense and, for previous actions, the present perfect. Of course, the past tense is appropriate in specific cases that clearly describe a past action. Aside from these particular cases, be sure to use the present and present perfect tenses consistently throughout the document.

> **Example:** In her autobiography *An American Childhood,* Annie Dillard beautifully **expresses** the feelings a child **has** as she gradually **becomes** aware of the exciting outside world surrounding her safe and familiar family life. Even though Dillard **wrote** and **published** this book when she was 42, she **has** realistically **recreated** the emotions of a young child.

Discussion: Verb Tense

Read aloud this introduction to a summary of an article from *The New Yorker* titled "Speed." The author, Dr. Oliver Sacks, writes "A Neurologist's Notebook" on medical subjects for this weekly magazine. After you underline the verbs, have a class discussion of the tenses used in this paragraph.

> In "Speed," by the well-known neurologist Oliver Sacks, (*The New Yorker,* August 23, 2004, 60–69), the author discusses how humans experience time and space, which has become a popular topic to psychologists. He analyzes the different perceptions that people have of time, the influence of drugs on our sense of time, and the effects that diseases can have, making the passage of time seem amazingly fast or horribly slow to the ill person. Sacks remembers that when he was a boy, the time passed extremely slowly because he "hated school, being forced to listen passively to droning teachers" (62). Apparently, boredom makes us pay particular attention to time: "indeed, when one is bored there may be no consciousness of anything *but* time" (Sacks 63). According to Sacks, human beings are "limited in speed" by our basic neurological structure (69), operating within a narrow range of physical and mental speed. Thus, researchers should conduct further experiments on this subject, using the virtual reality of computer simulation to speed up or slow down normal human reactions.

Paraphrasing

The goal of paraphrasing is to create an accurate restatement of the author's original words. In fact, being able to translate an author's words into your own words, without changing the intended meaning, is the most challenging aspect of writing a summary. This difficult skill depends on having competence in grammar and sentence structure, an extensive vocabulary, and an in-depth understanding of the author's ideas and purpose. The author's tone is also an essential element in paraphrasing: Is the author using persuasion, humor, irony, or anger to get the message across? If so, this tone should be part of your summary.

As you paraphrase the central ideas and conclusions in the original document, you should use the phrases, *according to Sacks, Sacks says, Sacks believes*; however, do not overuse these phrases in your summary. After you present the author's full name in your first paragraph, the reader understands that the author of the original document is the originator of all the ideas in the summary and doesn't need a reminder in every sentence. Also, use only the author's last name throughout the rest of the summary.

When paraphrasing, make sure that you have done a complete, not a partial, paraphrase. In a complete paraphrase, you transform the sentence structure, and you substitute synonyms for the original words without changing the meaning of the original statement. However, you should not change any technical terms, such as *analog*, because of their highly specific meaning. Although a summary is written as a paraphrase of the original material, you may include a few quotations that are particularly important to the meaning of the text or are unusually effective expressions that you could not recreate.

✓ PARAPHRASING TASK

Write complete paraphrases for the sentences on page 86 from "Other People's Words" by Paul Gray (*Smithsonian*, March 2002), which begins on page 87.

Example of a complete paraphrase

Original: "That Ambrose and Goodwin have offered readers some ostensibly original sentences that are not of their own is assuredly a lapse rather than a crime."

Paraphrase: When Ambrose and Goodwin included statements from other writers in their books without acknowledgment, it was certainly a minor mistake, not a criminal offense.

1. "Imagine yourself a high school history teacher who has been handed a research paper on air combat during World War II by one of your better students."

2. "If you decide that sloppiness is the cause, you flunk the paper and hope the lesson will stick, this time."

3. "If you have reasons to believe that deceit was the motive, you report your student to the responsible school authorities."

4. "Given Ambrose's prominence—he's appeared in photographs flanked by Tom Hanks and Steven Spielberg—the hunt was immediately on for other examples of apparent plagiarism in his works."

5. "Ambrose hadn't said he'd been careless through haste, but that, by his lights, he hadn't been careless at all."

6. "Other accusations of plagiarism have dragged prominent names through headlines with inconclusive results."

7. "Is any of this of more than academic interest?"

8. "These talented, industrious historians did not plagiarize their way into eminence."

9. "Unintentional theft remains theft, whether committed by those who know better or by those who are in the process of learning."

10. "Though some writers may shrug it off as the sincerest form of flattery, plagiarism is hardly a minor menace."

——————— **EVALUATION: "OTHER PEOPLE'S WORDS"** ———————

Using the **Preview, Read, Review** method, read the article on plagiarism titled "Other People's Words" by Paul Gray. Then read the summary of this article (pages 90–91), complete these tasks, and evaluate the summary with your classmates:

- Put brackets around the main idea in Gray's article.
- Highlight the major points in Gray's article.
- Underline the sentences in the article that are paraphrased in the summary.
- Underline the phrases and sentences in the article that are quoted in the summary.
- Circle the verb tenses the summary writer uses.

Summary Evaluation

Excellent +	Satisfactory √	Unsatisfactory –
• Reading comprehension		_____
• Critical analysis		_____
• Verb tenses		_____
• Paraphrasing		_____
• Citation of sources		_____

Other People's Words[4]

Though some writers may shrug it off as the sincerest form of flattery, plagiarism is hardly a minor menace

———————————

PAUL GRAY

Imagine yourself a high school history teacher who has been handed a research paper on air combat during World War II by one of your better students. In it, you come upon the following sentence, without quotation marks: "No amount of practice could have prepared the

---

[4] Paul Gray, "Other People's Words," *Smithsonian*, March 2002, 102–3.

pilot and crew for what they encountered—B-24s, glittering like mica, were popping up out of the clouds over here, over there, everywhere." A footnote identifies your student's source: *Wings of Morning* (1995), by Thomas Childers, page 83. You're conscientious about your work, so you check the reference against the Childers book, where you read: "No amount of practice could have prepared them for what they encountered. B-24s, glittering like mica, were popping up out of the clouds all over the sky."

Since it boggles the notion of probability to believe that these nearly identical sentences could have been written independently, you, dear teacher, are stuck with two possible explanations: either your student forgot the rule that the use of someone else's language must be identified as such by quotation marks—that is, that a footnote alone is not enough to indicate a word-for-word appropriation of material—or the student assumed that you wouldn't bother to track down the original passage. If you decide that sloppiness is the cause, you flunk the paper and hope the lesson will stick, this time; if you have reasons to believe that deceit was the motive, you report your student to the responsible school authorities.

But what should be the response when the malefactor isn't a teenager but rather Stephen E. Ambrose, 66, who has become . . . probably the most famous and widely read historian in the United States? For, as the *Weekly Standard* reports in early January 2002, Ambrose's best-selling *The Wild Blue* (2001) reproduced, footnoted but without quotation marks, the "glittering like mica" passage cited above, and two others as well, from Thomas Childers' book. Given Ambrose's prominence—he's appeared in photographs flanked by Tom Hanks and Steven Spielberg—the hunt was immediately on for other examples of apparent plagiarism in his works. Sure enough, other examples turned up: passages in *The Wild Blue* that are suspiciously similar to two other sources in addition to Childers, plus unacknowledged quotations in at least three of Ambrose's earlier books dating back to *Crazy Horse and Custer* in 1975.

A front-page story in *The New York Times* reporting the growing furor over Ambrose's methods included a truculent mea culpa by the historian: "I wish I had put quotation marks in, but I didn't. I am not out there stealing other people's writings. If I am writing up a passage and it is a story I want to tell and this story fits and a part of it is from other people's writing, I just type it up that way and put in a footnote. I just want to know where the hell it came from." This explanation baffled most academic historians, not to mention most readers of it. Even those who had defended Ambrose on the grounds that the former professor—with the help of his five grown children—churns out bestselling books so rapidly that slipshod mistakes were inevitable had to reconsider. Ambrose hadn't said he'd been careless through haste, but that, by his lights, he hadn't been careless at all.

While the Ambrose story still percolated in late January, the *Weekly Standard* (yes, again) published some passages from Doris Kearns Goodwin's *The Fitzgeralds and the Kennedys* (1987) that, without quotation marks, almost exactly reproduce passages in three earlier books about the Kennedys. Asked to comment on these similarities, Goodwin, whose book on Franklin and Eleanor Roosevelt won the 1995 Pulitzer Prize for history, told the *Weekly Standard:* "I wrote everything in longhand in those days, including the notes I took on secondary sources . . . Drawing on my notes, I did not realize that in some cases they constituted a close paraphrase of the original work."

Yep, that is certainly one way of committing what looks like plagiarism, and it's a way that beginning students are repeatedly reminded not to take.

What, if anything, should the reading public make of the Ambrose and Goodwin dustups or the many similar cases of plagiarism-spotting, real or fanciful, that have cropped up so often over the past few decades? Some have had real consequences. Alex Haley paid author Harold Courlander some $600,000 to settle a plagiarism suit for material Haley appropriated for *Roots* . . . ; Senator Joseph Biden's bid for the Democratic presidential nomination in 1988 hit a wall when it was demonstrated that he'd lifted a stump speech, virtually verbatim, from British Labour Party leader Neil Kinnock. Other accusations of plagiarism have dragged prominent names through headlines with inconclusive results: historian Stephen B. Oates, authors Susan Sontag and Jay McInerney. Is any of this of more than academic interest?

Certainly, if you believe that an author's words unencumbered by quotation marks have been conceived of and arranged solely by that author. This notion has been around long enough, one would think, for all concerned to have gotten the hang of it.

"Original" used to mean what it still means in the term "original sin": it's not a brand-new way of being evil but a reference to the stain of mortality engendered by the illicit apple tasting in the Garden of Eden. In the preface to his *Fables, Ancient and Modern* (1700), poet John Dryden apparently struck the word's modern coinage: "I have added some original papers of my own."

That Ambrose and Goodwin have offered readers some ostensibly orig- inal sentences that are not of their own is assuredly a lapse rather than a crime. These talented, industrious historians did not plagiarize their way into eminence. But the lapses remain troubling, as do the rather blithe, dis- missive self-defenses expressed by both authors. Unintentional theft remains theft, whether committed by those who know better or by those who are in the process of learning.

Summary

"Other People's Words"

OLIVIER CAVAGNA

In the article "Other People's Words" (*Smithsonian*, March 2002), Paul Gray argues that even when plagiarism is not done intentionally, it remains an immoral act, and, therefore, should not be downplayed. Teachers may be confronted with students who plagiarize because they have not learned the rule about inserting quotation marks when using someone else's language. However, well- known authors who should know better also plagiarize other people's material, which is unethical and unaccept- able behavior, according to Gray.

The author gives examples of recent cases where pla- giarism has been uncovered. He begins with Stephen

Ambrose, the historian who used other people's work in his books without acknowledging it. Ambrose didn't seem to think that he had been careless and was not particularly worried about his actions: "I wish I had put the quotation marks in, but I didn't" (Gray 102). Another case of plagiarism is Doris Kearns Goodwin, whose book *The Fitzgeralds and the Kennedys* contained passages taken from three earlier books on the Kennedys. Goodwin tried to justify her error by saying that she had not realized what she was doing. She also put the blame on writing in longhand rather than on a computer.

Serious consequences can occur if a person is caught plagiarizing. For example, Alex Haley, the author of *Roots*, had to pay $600,000 to Harold Courlander because Haley's book contained material from Courlander's book. This costly settlement reveals that plagiarism should be taken very seriously.

Gray raises a question: "Is any of this of more than academic interest?" (103). He answers this question by explaining what the word *original* means in its modern use: an author's own words and ideas. Gray concludes that although Ambrose and Goodwin's plagiarism may be considered "a lapse rather than a crime," it is a major error in ethical behavior: "intentional theft remains theft, whether committed by those who know better or by those who are in the process of learning" (103).

Works Cited

Gray, Paul. "Other People's Words." *Smithsonian* March 2002: 102–3.

 **ASSIGNMENT** | **Summary**

Do research on the Internet to locate a recent article on the subject of plagiarism, and write a summary of the article. Your summary should be about one-third the length of the original document. Attach a copy of your article to the summary when you hand it in. Remember to place the main idea of the article in the first paragraph, paraphrase the language of the original document, and write with objectivity.

Peer Critique

When you finish your first draft, exchange papers (including your articles) with a classmate, and evaluate your summaries using the Peer Critique Form.

Peer Critique

Evaluator _____

Author _____

Use this form to evaluate your classmate's summary. Mark the document as Excellent (E), Satisfactory (S), or Unsatisfactory (U) in each of the following categories:

- Grammar   correct standard English   _____
- Mechanics   correct punctuation, capitalization, spelling   _____
- Organization   logical and coherent presentation of ideas   _____
- Content   accurate and objective, with effective paraphrasing   _____
- Format   appropriate and consistent presentation on the page   _____
- Documentation   accurate and sufficient citation of sources   _____

Overall Evaluation _____

Comments

CHAPTER 8

The Logical Essay

An essay is an analytical or interpretative composition that deals with its subject in a limited way. It may be completely objective and based on research, contain the writer's opinion and personal experience, or be a combination of personal experience and research. Writing an essay can be done efficiently if the writer takes a systematic approach to the writing task by using the Power Writing Process, which was first described in Chapter 2 (page 12). This process includes five steps:

- **P**repare
- **O**utline
- **W**rite
- **E**dit
- **R**ewrite

STRATEGIES

Organization

In the United States most academic essays are organized in a linear pattern in which ideas are developed logically. The **introduction** contains background information and the thesis (main idea), followed by several **body** paragraphs, each discussing one major point that supports the thesis. The **conclusion** summarizes the major points and usually restates the thesis. Placing the thesis in the introduction is called **deductive** organization and is the preferred approach in academic writing, along with **deductive restatement,** with the thesis repeated in the conclusion. Papers may also be organized according to **inductive** organization, which involves presenting the thesis in the conclusion, rather than in the introduction, but this pattern is not common.

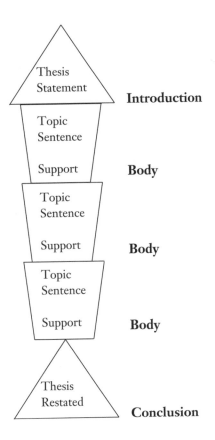

Personal Analytical Essay

When writing an essay that is centered on your personal experiences, make certain that you include specific details and vivid examples that support your thesis and major points. It is easy to forget the need for specificity and write in generalities, assuming that your reader will understand your ideas. This is a common mistake that essay writers make because they know their subject so well. But the reader wants the writer to fill in the blanks in the story and make all the logical connections explicit. The personal analytical essay has a subjective style and is less formal than the research essay. Thus, first person pronouns *(I and we)*, contractions *(I'll, can't, didn't)*, and idiomatic language are acceptable in most cases.

Research Essay

Writing a research essay requires you to maintain your focus on the purpose of your paper. Otherwise, you might get distracted while looking through books, articles, and websites in order to find the most relevant and reliable information for your essay. You must also remember to cite the source of all the information that you quote and/or paraphrase in the document. When doing Internet research, you should become adept at evaluating Internet sources to determine their value and validity. Because there are no standards that ensure accuracy, websites vary widely in their usefulness. Duke University provides an excellent explanation of how to evaluate websites: *www.lib.duke.edu/libguide/evaluating_web.htm#support/.*

The research essay incorporates a formal academic style and tone that are objective and impersonal. First-person pronouns *(I and we)*, contractions *(I'll, can't, didn't)*, and idiomatic language are generally avoided. (See Chapter 5, Effective Style, and Appendix B, Examples of Writing Styles.) The goal is to produce a document that meets the criteria of academic writing: substantive content, sound mechanics, logical organization, effective style, and accurate documentation.

Introduction and Thesis

The introduction to an essay presents the thesis (main idea), establishes the style and tone, and develops a context for the essay. It usually moves from statements of general information to specific statements, so you can visualize the introductory paragraph as an inverted pyramid, with the precisely stated main idea as the last sentence. The sentences preceding the thesis should familiarize the reader with background on the topic and set the stage for the rest of the essay. When you are writing a personal analytical essay, construct the background information so that it leads naturally to a subjectively stated thesis. If you are writing a research essay, discuss the goal and context of your research and conclude with an objectively stated thesis.

Conclusion

In a conclusion, you should summarize the major points of the essay and restate the thesis, using paraphrased language. A relevant quotation is an effective technique that makes the conclusion memorable, and sometimes the writer may predict a future course of action or offer a general solution if the essay has centered on a problem. A conclusion will be weak or ineffective if you add new and unrelated information or don't make the concluding paragraph long enough. A conclusion should be about the same length as the other paragraphs in the essay in order to create a balanced and well-designed document.

Citation Style

Writers have to differentiate between their original work and the ideas and words that belong to other writers. The method to do this is called **citation (attribution) of sources.** Attributions are given in the text immediately after the borrowed words, phrases, and sentences or are footnoted at the bottom of a page. These sources must all be listed at the end of a document under the headings Works Cited, References, or Bibliography. The sources are alphabetized according to the author's last name. If no author is identified, they are alphabetized by the first word of the title, not including *a, an,* or *the.*

Each academic field has its own style of citation. The Modern Language Association (MLA) style for citation is preferred for papers written in the humanities. (The APA style is more common in the social and behavioral sciences.) In MLA style, the author's last name and the page number where the information is located are inserted within parentheses in the text: (Lowell 258).

These cases need to be cited:

- Quotations of the exact words, phrases, and sentences from the work of another person
- Paraphrases or summaries of the ideas of others
- Facts and statistics from various sources
- Information from Internet sources such as websites, online journals, and newspapers
- Graphic aids (charts, graphs, photographs, film stills) from various sources
- Ideas from lectures, speeches, or classroom discussions
- Dialogue from movies and plays

Duke University provides a Guide to Library Research with comprehensive information about citation rules under Citing Sources (Citing Sources and Avoiding Plagiarism: Documentation Guidelines) at *www.lib.duke.edu/libguide/.*

For the rules on citation of electronic sources, see Citation Styles: Using MLA Style to Cite and Document Sources in Online! at *www.bedfordstmartins.com/online/cite5.html*.

———— ANALYSIS: "PART-TIME WORKERS IN JAPAN" ————

The Personal Analytical Essay is developed from an analysis of the writer's experiences. Depending on the topic and assignment, outside sources and research may be necessary. The Research Essay is built on outside sources and requires research. Of course, many documents are based on a combination of personal experience and research. After reading "Part-Time Women Workers in Japan" (pages 99–100) and "Major Differences between English and Japanese" (pages 101-103), complete these tasks. Then evaluate the essays with your classmates using the form below.

- Put brackets around the thesis (main idea) of the essay.
- Underline the topic sentence in each paragraph.
- Put brackets around the supporting facts, statistics, examples, and quotations in each paragraph.
- Underline the closing or bridge sentence in each paragraph.
- Highlight the pronouns, contractions, and idiomatic language.
- Highlight the verbs.

Essay Evaluation		
Excellent +	**Satisfactory √**	**Unsatisfactory −**
• Format		_____
• Organization		_____
• Content		_____
• Understanding of topic		_____
• Style		_____
• Citation of sources		_____

Research Essay

Part-Time Women Workers in Japan

KIYOSHI TAKEDA

The Japanese Equal Employment Opportunity Law for Men and Women came into effect in April 1986 in Japan. This law "required companies to make efforts not to discriminate on the basis of sex" (Shinotsuka). The law was revised in June 1997 to speed up measures to counteract male-female discrimination. The revised law prohibits gender-based discrimination in job recruitment, employment, allocation of specific posts, and job advancement. Although the law was created almost twenty years ago and recently revised, it has not made everyone equal before the law. The employment opportunities for Japanese men and women are still not equal: many Japanese women are employed as part-timers and paid lower salaries than men (Women's Working Conditions).

The number of working women in Japan has increased slightly in recent years, but more than one-third of them work on a part-time basis. In 1980, 21.4 million workers were women, in 1999, 26.3 million women worked, and in 2000, 27.9 million women worked. Thus, 41 percent of the Japanese workforce of 68 million was made up of women in 2000 (www.worldbank. org). However, Japanese women have faced difficulty in getting stable jobs since Japan's "bubble economy" ended in 1992 and Japan entered an economic recession. Because Japanese companies seek to hire low-wage part-time employees, 8.35 million women are employed as part-timers today (Kakuchi). Full-time female workers are mostly young women who are fresh out of college. Japanese companies demand long working hours and employee loyalty, so these young women usually quit their jobs when they start their families. If they want to work at the company as full-time workers again, after their children are in school, there is no way to do so. Therefore, they often have to look for part-time jobs (Kakuchi).

Japanese women have traditionally been paid lower salaries than men for doing the same job. The Japanese Labor Ministry statistics reveal the following facts: the average salary for women in 2001 was 65.3 percent that of men, compared with a gap of 76 percent in the United States and 80.6 percent in Britain in 1991. Women part-timers are mostly employed in factories and in service sectors such as supermarkets, restaurants, and hotels. They work long hours and are paid less than men in these service jobs. Since Japanese companies are interested in saving money, and women are reliable employees, they prefer to hire part-time women workers (Kakuchi).

According to an expert in business administration, the Japanese employment system should be overhauled. This expert says: "The reason why women, while ambitious, have stayed away from pursuing careers is because they cannot meet the conditions applied to climbing up the career ladder" (Kakuchi). Moreover, some companies exploit their women workers. Currently the government is taking steps to crack down on unpaid overtime for part-timers, a regular practice in most companies. Shorter working hours are also being proposed. In fact, Japanese companies have recently developed new benefit systems that seem to address the needs of women (including part-timers) more than those of men (Women's Working Conditions). Perhaps in the future the Japanese government will encourage companies to revise their labor laws so that women can have the same employment opportunities as men. However, "cultural and historical factors" have slowed the rate of change in the Japanese workforce (Shinotsuka).

Works Cited

"Japan." World Bank Group. 2005. < http://www.worldbank.org >.

Kakuchi, Suvendrini. "Labor-Japan: Women Part-Timers Gain amid Workplace Changes." Global Information Network. 15 Jan. 2004.

Shinotsuka, Eiko. "Working Women in Japan." AskAsia. 2003. Asia Society. 10 Feb. 2005. < http://www.askasia.org >. (Search for Working Women in Japan.)

"Women's Working Conditions." Web Japan. Japanese Ministry of Foreign Affairs. 10 Feb. 2005. <http://www.web-japan.org>.

CHAPTER 9

The Objective Critical Review

A **critical review** is a paper in which writers offer a reasoned response to the argument that an author has presented in an article or a book. Other names for a critical review are **critique** and **reaction paper,** and such documents also evaluate films, plays, musical performances, art, and architecture. In a critical review of an article or book, writers express an overall opinion in the introduction and summarize the author's argument. Then they evaluate the author's ideas, data, or conclusions according to specific criteria, such as logic, accuracy, objectivity, and timeliness. Critical reviews come in many forms, with varying degrees of formality, ranging from informal movie reviews to formal reviews of research studies in scientific journals. Similar to a summary, a critical review is written in the present and present perfect tense, with the exception of using the past tense for specific individual past actions.

This format is suggested for writing a critical review.

I. Introduction
   A. Background information about the author and topic
   B. Thesis (the writer's evaluation of the author's argument)

II. Summary of article or book
   A. Major points
   B. Supporting points

III. Critique
   A. Analysis of the author's argument
   B. Agreement or disagreement with the author's argument

IV. Conclusion
   A. Summary
   B. Restatement of thesis

--- **STRATEGIES** ---

Thesis

When you are reviewing a book or movie, the thesis may be a general assessment of the entire work. However, when you are reviewing an article or book chapter, the thesis contains your unbiased evaluation of the argument, evidence, or suggestions proposed by an author. You can arrive at this evaluation by critically examining the document in light of various criteria, including, but not limited to, reliability of data, logic of reasoning, justification for conclusion, viability of suggestion, objectivity of assessment, originality of proposal, or credibility of the author. In your thesis, you should clearly state the grounds on which you are judging the document so the reader can understand the reasoning behind your decision. Write your thesis in an objective, factual, balanced manner, using the present or present perfect verb tenses.

Examples of Theses for Critical Reviews

Although Karen Field makes a compelling argument for home schooling, she does not provide sufficient evidence for her claim that home-schooled children score higher on standardized tests than students who attend traditional schools.

Robert Martelli presents a variety of psychological theories to support his proposal that marijuana should be legalized; however, his argument is weak in logic and lacks objective evidence.

While the author has assembled a strongly argued case for abolishing capital punishment, his argument that capital punishment is not a deterrent to crime is unsupported by recent data.

Analytical Reading

Writing an objective, balanced critical review reveals your competence not only in writing and critical thinking but also in reading. To understand the subtleties of an author's point of view and analyze the material thoughtfully, you should use the method of active reading—Preview, Read, Review—discussed in Chapter 7.

This method involves first **previewing** the reading to get a general impression of the content and organization. Next, you **read** the document carefully, interacting with the ideas and responding to them by annotating (making comments on) the text. You should underline topic sentences, key terms, and supporting data, and write comments or question marks in the margin to show your agreement or disagreement with the author. Finally, you read the document a third time, **reviewing** your earlier comments and questions, circling new vocabulary words, and highlighting any phrases or sentences that are not clear or convincing so that you can return to the passage later.

Analytical reading is a two-track thinking process in which an experienced reader simultaneously decodes the meaning of the words and assesses the value of the content, questioning the author's methods, data, and conclusions. Is the author qualified to address this topic? How does the author build the case or construct the proposal? What evidence supports the conclusions? Does the author use facts or opinions, generalizations or specifics? What do other experts on the topic have to say about this author's ideas? Does the author have a bias? Is the document well written, creative, and readable? You should be thinking about these questions and annotating the material as you read and reread the article or book.

Evaluation Criteria

Evaluating the strengths and weaknesses of an author's ideas is a challenging task that demands a high level of critical thinking from the reviewer. The best critical review will reveal an objective, unbiased approach in which the writer applies several specific criteria to a book or article and arrives at a reasonable assessment based on evidence. This assessment could be entirely positive, entirely negative, or a combination of positive and negative. In thinking critically about what you are reading, you *investigate* the author's logic; *analyze and synthesize* information; *draw inferences; form interpretations*; and *question* the author's methods, conclusions, or beliefs.

You must select from the article or book the major point(s) that you wish to address in your review because attempting to write too much will dilute the focus of your review. Your evaluation could assess the ideas, the evidence, the writing itself, or a combination of these factors. In the columns, negative words that apply to ideas, evidence, or writing are listed. Discuss with your classmates the positive words that go with each negative word.

Criticism of Ideas	Criticism of Evidence	Criticism of Writing
illogical	insufficient	unclear
unrealistic	biased	incoherent
not viable	out of date	redundant
unjustified	unverifiable	imprecise
unsupported	irrelevant	disorganized
unoriginal	distorted	not specific
unprofessional	unconvincing	inaccurate
simplistic	ambiguous	inconsistent

Academic Style

A critical review is characterized by a formal academic style, which is largely determined by the word choice; for example, the writer uses poly-syllabic words such as *assistance* rather than *help* or *demonstrate* rather than *show.* In addition, the review could contain technical language, depending on the topic of the review. First-person pronouns (*I, we*) and second-person pronouns (*you*) are avoided; instead, the reviewer uses the third person (*he, she, it, they*) to create an objective style. Contractions and idiomatic language are not appropriate in a critical review. The overall tone is impersonal, bal-anced, and factual, and this tone should be consistent throughout the docu-ment. In a reaction paper, which differs slightly from a critical review or critique, the style and tone may be somewhat subjective, as the writer is pre-senting his or her personal response to an author's ideas. Thus, a thesis could be written in the first-person: *I find Goodwin's justification of her citation errors unconvincing.*

A critical review usually contains citation of sources and Works Cited. Each academic field has its own style of citation. This textbook suggests the use of the MLA style for citation, which is generally preferred for papers written in the humanities, including English and foreign languages. In MLA style, you insert the author's last name and the page number within paren-theses following the quotation or paraphrase: (Lowell 258). List all your sources at the end of your paper under Works Cited, alphabetizing them by the author's last name. If no author is identified, alphabetize the sources by the first word of the title, not including *a, an,* or *the.*

Formal Style: Word Choice

A formal style generally results from the use of complex, polysyllabic words, while an informal style is created by the use of short and simple words. Single verbs, in particular, are more formal than two-word verbs. For example, *choose* conveys formality, while *pick out* conveys informality.

The lists on page 110 contain formal words and their informal equiva-lents. Read the explanation of the Power Writing Process that follows on pages 111–112. Then, working with a partner, fill in the blanks with the cor-rect words on the lists. (You will need 16 words.) One partner should use only the formal words, and the other should use only the informal words. After you complete the paragraphs, compare them and discuss how these paragraphs differ in style and tone.

Formal	Informal
anticipate	expect
assistance	help
approximately	about
choose	pick out
component	part
consider	think of, about
cooperate	work together
currently	now
demonstrate	show
determine	find out
difficult	hard
endeavor	try
enhance	make better
examine	look over
facilitate	make easy
finalize	finish
identify	find
indicate	show
initial	first
initiate	begin
insufficient	not enough
modification	change
prioritize	rank
reconsider	think about again
request	ask for
require	need
reveal	show
review	check
state	say
submit	give
subsequently	later
substantial	great, big
sufficient	enough
terminate	end
transform	change
utilize	use

The Power Writing Process

To improve writing skills, writers should ___utilize / endeavor___ writing as an analytical process with five distinct ___Components___: preparing, outlining, writing, editing, and rewriting. In the preparation stage, writers can clarify their purpose, audience, and goal. They should also ___indicate___ whether they have ___Sufficient___ knowledge about their topic or will have to do research to ___examine___ sources and gather information.

With an outline, writers can ___facilitate___ their information by constructing a thesis, major and minor points, and supporting data, such as facts, statistics, examples, and quotations. Following an outline ___Prioritize___ the actual writing because the outline functions as a roadmap that efficiently guides writers to their logical destination.

In the writing stage, writers ___enhance___ their outlined thoughts into pages of paragraphs after they decide which style and tone would be appropriate for their purpose and audience. This is the most ___difficult___ part of the process for many writers, whose ___inital___ draft may not be clear, concise, or coherent.

Having completed the first draft, authors must ___demonstrate___ their editing ability to ___Cooperate___ and enhance the content, style, and organization of their documents. Skillful editing can involve a ___insufficient___ amount of time. It ___requires___ concentration on all aspects of the document, including proofreading for grammar and punctuation errors.

This is the time to _____review_____ the document's clarity and coherence as evidenced by its readability. The final step is to rewrite the first draft, incorporating _____ from the editing stage and ensuring that citations of sources, if necessary, are accurate.

Evaluation: "How I Caused That Story"

Read the article "How I Caused That Story" (*Time*, February 4, 2002), which begins on page 113, in which historian Doris Kearns Goodwin responds to charges of plagiarism and explains her citation errors. Two critical reviews (pages 115–18) present opposing viewpoints on her response. Which of these two reviews do you find the most convincing? Why?

After reading both reviews, complete these tasks, and evaluate the reviews with your classmates.

- Put brackets around the thesis (main idea) of the critical review.
- Highlight the evaluation criteria the writer uses.
- Underline the topic sentence in each paragraph.
- Put brackets around the supporting facts, statistics, examples, and quotations in each paragraph.
- Underline the evaluative statements in the review, noting if they are positive or negative.
- Highlight all pronouns.
- Highlight all verbs, adjectives, and adverbs.

How I Caused That Story[1]

A historian explains why someone else's writing wound up in her book

---

DORIS KEARNS GOODWIN

I am a historian. With the exception of being a wife and mother, it is who I am. And there is nothing I take more seriously.

In recent days, questions have been raised about how historians go about crediting their sources, and I have been caught up in the swirl. Ironically, the more intensive and far-reaching a historian's research, the greater the difficulty of citation. As the mountain of material grows, so does the possibility of error.

Fourteen years ago, not long after the publication of my book *The Fitzgeralds and the Kennedys*, I received a communication from author Lynne McTaggart pointing out that material from her book on Kathleen Kennedy had not been properly attributed. I realized that she was right. Though my footnotes repeatedly cited Ms. McTaggart's work, I failed to provide quotation marks for phrases that I had taken verbatim, having assumed that these phrases, drawn from my notes, were my words, not hers. I made the corrections she requested, and the matter was completely laid to rest—until last week, when the *Weekly Standard* published an article reviving the issue. The larger question for those of us who write history is to understand how citation mistakes can happen.

The research and writing for this 900-page book, with its 3,500 footnotes, took place over 10 years. At that time, I wrote my books and took my notes in longhand, believing I could not think well on a keyboard. Most of my sources were drawn from a multitude of primary materials: manuscript collections, private letters, diaries, oral histories, newspapers, periodicals, personal interviews. After three years of research, I discovered more than 150 cartons of materials that had been previously stored in the attic of Joe Kennedy's Hyannis Port House. These materials were a treasure trove for a historian—old report cards, thousands of family letters, movie stubs and diaries, which allowed me to cross the boundaries of time and space. It took me two additional years to read, categorize and take notes on these documents.

---

[1] Doris Kearns Goodwin, "How I Caused That Story," *Time*, February 4, 2002, 69.

During this same period, I took handwritten notes on perhaps 300 books. Passages I wanted to quote directly were noted along with general notes on the ideas and story lines of each book. Notes on all these sources were then arranged chronologically and kept in dozens of folders in 25 banker's boxes. Immersed in a flood of papers, I began to write the book. After each section and each chapter was completed, I returned the notes to the boxes along with notations for future footnoting. When the manuscript was finished, I went back to all these sources to check the accuracy of attributions. As a final protection, I revisited the 300 books themselves. Somehow in this process, a few of the books were not fully rechecked. I relied instead on my notes, which combined direct quotes and paraphrased sentences. If I had had the books in front of me, rather than my notes, I would have caught the mistakes in the first place and placed any borrowed phrases in direct quotes.

What made this incident particularly hard for me was the fact that I take great pride in the depth of my research and the extensiveness of my citations. The writing of history is a rich process of building on the work of the past with the hope that others will build on what you have done.

Through footnotes you point the way to future historians.

The only protection as a historian is to institute a process of research and writing that minimizes the possibility of error. And that I have tried to do, aided by modern technology, which enables me, having long since moved beyond longhand, to use a computer for both organizing and taking notes. I now rely on a scanner, which reproduces the passages I want to cite, and then I keep my own comments on those books in a separate file so that I will never confuse the two again. But the real miracle occurred when my college-age son taught me how to use the mysterious footnote key on the computer, which makes it possible to insert the citations directly in the text while the sources are still in front of me, instead of shuffling through hundreds of folders four or five years down the line, trying desperately to remember from where I derived a particular statistic or quote. Still, there is no guarantee against error. Should one occur, all I can do, as I did 14 years ago, is to correct it as soon as I possibly can, for my own sake and the sake of history. In the end, I am still the same fallible person I was before I made the transition to the computer, and the process of building a lengthy work of history remains a complicated but honorable task.

Critical Review Evaluation

Excellent +	Satisfactory √	Unsatisfactory −
• Format		_____
• Organization		_____
• Content		_____
• Understanding of topic		_____
• Style		_____
• Citation of sources		_____

Critical Review

"How I Caused That Story"

Misako Schreim

In the article "How I Caused That Story," which appeared in *Time* (February 4, 2002), Doris Kearns Goodwin explains how she unintentionally plagiarized in one of her books fourteen years ago. Because of the significant number of reference materials needed for her complicated historical research, she says that the possibility of error was great. Moreover, there is no guarantee that she will not make an error again, even though she is now using a computer to avoid mistakes. Her explanation makes her errors seem understandable. However, if a professional historian is allowed to make these citation mistakes, historical information will not be accurate for future reference. Moreover, as a professional historian, she must take responsibility for using citations correctly and in accordance with U.S. copyright laws. Therefore, her explanation about her plagiarism sounds somewhat unprofessional and is not convincing.

According to Goodwin, after she published *The Fitzgeralds and the Kennedys*, she was accused of plagiarism, which she claimed happened by mistake. Goodwin explains that the 900-page book, which she wrote over a ten-year period, had 3,500 footnotes based on 300 reference books. She had taken an enormous number of notes by hand, and she checked the accuracy of her sources carefully, but somehow she confused her paraphrased sentences with direct quotes taken from another author: "If I had had the books in front of me, rather than my notes, I would have caught mistakes in the first place and placed any borrowed phrases in direct quotes" (Goodwin 69). Goodwin believes that the only way to prevent plagiarism is to organize research materials by using computer technology. However, it is still possible to make an error, especially when a historian's research is complicated and lengthy (Goodwin 69).

A historian's work is complex, involving significant numbers of sources, in this case, 300 reference books and 3,500 footnotes. Nevertheless, when it comes to history, incomplete documentation is not acceptable. It is critical that historical writing contain accurate quotations and footnotes that will give additional meaning to the work under discussion. If a citation in historical writing is omitted, future historians will be confused, and the situation might cause questions about the historian's work. As a result, the historical record might be misinterpreted because of incorrect information. In other words, any piece of information about history should be cited correctly because correct evidence is essential.

Regarding rules related to her work as a professional writer, Goodwin should be aware of the importance of U.S. copyright laws, which prohibit a person from using someone else's writing as if it were his or hers. This is an ethical and legal issue regarding acknowledgement of and respect for other people's original work. In addition, Goodwin is paid for her work as a professional writer, so she should be held responsible for her work just like all paid employees have to take responsibility for fulfilling the requirements of their jobs.

Works Cited

Goodwin, Doris Kearns. "How I Caused That Story." *Time* 4 Feb. 2002: 69.

Critical Review

"How I Caused That Story"

DOMINIQUE FOTSO

In "How I Caused That Story" (*Time*, February 4, 2002), Doris Kearns Goodwin, a Pulitzer-prizewinning historian, tries to clarify how author Lynne McTaggart's writing appeared in her book *The Fitzgeralds and the Kennedys* without being correctly attributed. She describes the research process of a historian and concludes that mistakes are likely to happen in this kind of complicated work. Her explanation of her plagiarism, which emphasizes human fallibility, is a persuasive piece of writing.

In her article, Goodwin relates how the incident happened and takes responsibility for it. Fourteen years ago, after McTaggart complained that Goodwin used her language without quotation marks, Goodwin corrected the omissions, but in February 2002, the *Weekly Standard* reported the incident. As a consequence, she published this article describing the process of writing a historical book in order to convince readers that an error can easily occur. While writing *The Fitzgeralds and the Kennedys*, Goodwin read many materials, took notes, and classified them by source and author. She checked her footnotes against her sources to catch any mistakes. However, in this complex process, Goodwin did not get rid of every inaccuracy. She admits her fault but tries to make it appear less serious than some might think it is and says that now she uses computer technology to lessen the chance of errors.

Goodwin's explanation for her plagiarism is reasonable, according to my own experience. College students are assigned many essays with citations and references that require a great deal of work to be effective and without error. In fact, who has never made a mistake in doing this task? At the college level, it is hardly possible to do comprehensive research without making a single citation mistake. Thus, Goodwin's research, which was much more complex than college writing, required more effort and had a greater chance of errors. In addition, the author depended on her usual methodology in the research process, but she did not have modern computer technology to prevent mistakes from slipping into her work.

Furthermore, Goodwin has the impressive ability to persuade readers with her writing style. First of all, she admits her responsibility in this issue: "I failed to provide quotation marks for phrases that I had taken verbatim . . ." (Goodwin 69). More to the point, she uses many skillful methods to convey the immensity of a historian's research. She gives enormous numbers related to the project: "900-page book," "3,500 footnotes," "300 books," "thousands of family letters" (Goodwin 69). Also she uses several action verbs to illustrate the difficult work she has to do: take, read, categorize, revisit, arrange, recheck (Goodwin 69). The author shows us her talent in writing, and it contributes to the persuasive tone.

Goodwin strongly defends her position and explains how her plagiarism occurred. Admitting her responsibility and outlining the research process of a historian, she successfully clarifies the issue and justifies her actions. In the end, she describes herself as a "fallible person" (Goodwin 69), which is a reasonable depiction of any human being.

Works Cited

Goodwin, Doris Kearns. "How I Caused That Story." *Time* 4 Feb. 2002: 69.

ASSIGNMENT Critical Review

The immigration policy of the United States is a controversial topic. In 2002, the editor-in-chief of *U.S. News & World Report* wrote "Our Rainbow Underclass" (*U.S. News & World Report*, 23 September 2002), which discussed social and economic problems caused by the current policy.

Then, on January 7, 2004, President Bush proposed a change in the U.S. immigration policy that would give illegal immigrants with jobs the right to stay in the United States for three years and to renew their temporary worker status when the three years expire. In defense of that proposal, Mortimer B. Zuckerman, the editor-in-chief of *U.S. News & World Report*, wrote "Learning to Live with Others" (*U.S. News & World Report*, 26 January 2004).

Complete these tasks:

1. Read the critical review of "Our Rainbow Underclass," pages 120–21, which provides background information and can serve as a model for your review.
2. Read the press release on pages 122–25 from January 7, 2004: "President Bush Proposes New Temporary Worker Program: Remarks by the President on Immigration Policy."
3. Read "Learning to Live with Others" by Zuckerman on pages 126–128.
4. Write a 500-word critical review of "Learning to Live with Others."

Critical Review

"Our Rainbow Underclass"

JUNICHI NAGAI

In the article "Our Rainbow Underclass," which appeared in *U.S. News & World Report* (September 23, 2002), Mortimer B. Zuckerman, Editor-in-Chief, explains why recent immigrants to the United States a need long time to assimilate into American society and why their children form a rainbow underclass. In addition, he presents three suggestions to solve the problem of the rainbow underclass and asks for a national dialogue on immigration (Zuckerman 118). This article is interesting and informative. However, it is not objective because it is an editorial based on Zuckerman's opinion. His analysis is only from the viewpoint of native-born Americans' welfare and lacks perspective on recent immigrants' and their children's welfare. In addition, his analysis seems biased by ethnic prejudice.

According to Zuckerman's analysis, the Immigration Reform Act enacted in 1965 triggered an immigration explosion, which resulted in a huge inflow of Third World immigrants. As a result, traditional immigrants from northern and western Europe were discriminated against. Previous immigrants could find well-paid jobs and formed the middle class in the United States. In addition, they sent their children to high-quality urban schools, so their children's assimilation into American society was swift. On the other hand, recent immigrants, for instance, Latino immigrants, have poor or non-existent English ability and low-paying jobs. Thus, they have become an underclass in the United States (Zuckerman 118).

The children of recent immigrants, Zuckerman says, form "our rainbow underclass" (118). To Zuckerman a rainbow symbolizes the diversity in American society, but these children are an underclass, a group that is poor. The children of recent immigrants have been caught in a cycle of downward assimilation and have succumbed to the danger of an overcrowded inner-city culture. Therefore, the dropout rate of the second-generation children is three times as high as that of native-born Americans. Zuckerman introduces the results of studies that show Chinese students no longer exceed whites in educational success by the third generation (118). In addition, the high birth rate of these recent immigrants will cause incalculable problems from rush-hour traffic to air and water pollution and social tension.

Zuckerman offers three suggestions to solve these problems. The first suggestion is to make use of the schools and the other institutions to support the development of the second-generation children. The second is to revise the immigration law and promote immigrants with skills transferable to the information economy. The third is to slow down the immigration process until the lives of the children of today's immigrants can be restructured in a positive direction (Zuckerman 118).

Zuckerman's perspective is understandable, but his limited analysis seems biased by ethnic prejudice because it is only based on the data of immigrants who fail to assimilate into American society and offers no analysis of recent successful immigrants. The purpose of his suggestions seems to be to provide native-born Americans with problem-free lives. He lacks an understanding of the many immigrants and their children who have assimilated into American society while retaining their own ethnic identity. Zuckerman is too vigilant about protecting American society from non-European immigrants to think about coexistence with them.

Works Cited

Zuckerman, Mortimer B. "Our Rainbow Underclass." *U.S. News & World Report*, 23 Sept. 2002: 118.

President Bush Proposes New Temporary Worker Program[2]

Remarks by the President on Immigration Policy

I propose a new temporary worker program that will match willing foreign workers with willing American employers, when no Americans can be found to fill the jobs. This program will offer legal status, as temporary workers, to the millions of undocumented men and women now employed in the United States, and to those in foreign countries who seek to participate in the program and have been offered employment here. This new system should be clear and efficient, so employers are able to find workers quickly and simply.

All who participate in the temporary worker program must have a job, or, if not living in the United States, a job offer. The legal status granted by this program will last three years and will be renewable—but it will have an end. Participants who do not remain employed, who do not follow the rules of the program, or who break the law will not be eligible for continued participation and will be required to return to their home.

Under my proposal, employers have key responsibilities. Employers who extend job offers must first make every reasonable effort to find an American worker for the job at hand. Our government will develop a quick and simple system for employers to search for American workers. Employers must not hire undocumented aliens or temporary workers whose legal status has expired. They must report to the government the temporary workers they hire, and who leave their employ, so that we can keep track of people in the program, and better enforce immigration laws. There must be strong workplace enforcement with tough penalties for anyone, for any employer violating these laws.

Undocumented workers now here will be required to pay a one-time fee to register for the temporary worker program. Those who seek to join the program from abroad, and have complied with our immigration laws, will not have to pay any fee. All participants will be issued a temporary worker card that will allow them to travel back and forth between their home and the United States without fear of being denied re-entry into our country.

This program expects temporary workers to return permanently to their home countries after their period of work in the United States has expired. And there should be financial incentives for them to do so. I will work with foreign governments on a plan to give temporary workers credit, when they enter their own nation's retirement system, for the time they have worked in America. I also support making it easier for temporary workers to contribute a portion of their earnings to tax-preferred savings accounts, money they can collect as they return to their native countries. After all, in many of those countries, a small nest egg is what is necessary to start their own business, or buy some land for their family.

Some temporary workers will make the decision to pursue American citizenship. Those who make this choice will be allowed to apply in the normal way. They will not be given unfair advantage over people who have followed legal procedures from the start. I oppose amnesty, placing undocumented workers on the automatic path to citizenship. Granting amnesty encourages the violation of our laws and perpetuates illegal immigration. America is a welcoming country, but citizenship must not be the automatic reward for violating the laws of America.

The citizenship line, however, is too long, and our current limits on legal immigration are too low. My administration will work with the Congress to increase the annual number of green cards that can lead to citizenship. Those willing to take the difficult path of citizenship—the path of work, and patience, and assimilation—should be welcome in America, like generations of immigrants before them.

In the process of immigration reform, we must also set high expectations for what new citizens should know. An understanding of what it means to be an American is not a formality in the naturalization process; it is essential to full participation in our democracy. My administration will examine the standard of knowledge in the current citizenship test. We must ensure that new citizens know not only the facts of our history, but the ideals that have shaped our history. Every citizen of America has an obligation to learn the values that make us one nation: liberty and civic responsibility, equality under God, and tolerance for others.

This new temporary worker program will bring more than economic benefits to America. Our homeland will be more secure when we can better account for those who enter our country, instead of the current situation in which millions of people are unknown, unknown to the law. Law enforcement will face fewer problems with undocumented workers, and will be better able to focus on the true threats to our nation from criminals and terrorists. And when temporary workers can travel legally and freely, there will be more efficient management of our borders and more effective enforcement against those who pose a danger to our country.

This new system will be more compassionate. Decent, hard-working people will now be protected by labor laws, with the right to change jobs, earn fair wages, and enjoy the same working conditions that the law requires for American workers. Temporary workers will be able to establish their identities by obtaining the legal documents we all take for granted. And they will be able to talk openly to authorities, to report crimes when they are harmed, without the fear of being deported.

The best way, in the long run, to reduce the pressures that create illegal immigration in the first place is to expand economic opportunity among the countries in our neighborhood. In a few days I will go to Mexico for the Special Summit of the Americas, where we will discuss ways to advance free trade, and to fight corruption, and encourage the reforms that lead to prosperity. Real growth and real hope in the nations of our hemisphere will lessen the flow of new immigrants to America when more citizens of other countries are able to achieve their dreams at their own home.

Yet our country has always benefited from the dreams that others have brought here. By working hard for a better life, immigrants contribute to the life of our nation. The temporary worker program I am proposing today represents the best tradition of our society, a society that honors the law, and welcomes the newcomer. This plan will help return order and fairness to our immigration system, and in so doing we will honor our values, by showing our respect for those who work hard and share in the ideals of America.

Learning to Live with Others[3]

MORTIMER B. ZUCKERMAN, EDITOR-IN-CHIEF

Most Americans are deeply unhappy about immigration and troubled by President Bush's new program. In a *USA Today*/CNN/ Gallup Poll out this week, 55 percent opposed the plan, two thirds believe that immigrants hurt the economy by driving down wages for Americans, and 74 percent oppose making it easier for illegal immigrants to become citizens. That last number is up from 67 percent just two years ago. Many in the Hispanic community, on the other hand, regard the Bush plan as half a loaf and not the full amnesty program they seek.

There's no easy answer to the gravitational pull of the American job market that now has attracted somewhere between 10 million and 14 million undocumented workers—illegal immigrants whose numbers are growing at the rate of almost half a million people a year. They can make as much in half an hour as a migrant can make at home in a day. So they put up with conditions and wages that most Americans would never accept, to do work that needs to be done. This is a market force that will always overwhelm the obstacles to border jumping, a force that will only expand as the native labor force grows older and more middle-class workers will be even less willing to work as busboys and gardeners and in household services. Just what we have to face was brought home to me when, some 10 years ago, I spent a night with the Border Patrol in a helicopter flying along Texas-Mexico frontier. Thousands were captured every night and sent back, only to return again and again until they were able to evade the border patrols.

Honestly. America isn't going to deport this sub rosa population. We simply wouldn't take on the moral, political, and financial burden of expelling millions of people and disrupting or ruining the lives of millions of otherwise law-abiding, hardworking people. Immigration is, after all, the history of America. Yet, America cannot be a healthy society when there are so many mil-

---

[3] Mortimer B. Zuckerman, "Learning to Live with Others," *U.S. News & World Report*, January 26, 2004, 60.

lions of illegal immigrants living in the shadows, ignoring the law, and living under conditions that expose them to exploitation. Nor can we afford the luxury of a southern or even a northern border to be so loosely controlled while "coyote" networks smuggle in illegal immigrants in a pipeline that can also be used to ferry in terrorists and provide fake documents.

But if we can't stem the tide, what can we do to control it and minimize the bad consequences? President Bush's proposal has the merit of bringing honesty to the issue. Those now here who can prove they have a job and qualify to get work permits will have the right to work legally for three years, a right that could be renewed an unspecified number of times. It is essentially a guest-worker program that would feed the migrants into a legal channel where they become taxpayers and meet other obligations of citizenship.

Foreigners who have job offers from American employers that cannot be filled by Americans could also participate in this program. All would be able to travel back and forth to their native countries and not be precluded from applying for a green card, which grants them permanent residency. The president

also recognized that we must increase the number of green cards. If we don't, illegal immigrants who fear they might not receive a green card before their guest-worker status expires simply won't participate in the program.

The value of immigration can be seen everywhere: in the scientists and engineers who make up a third of the technical workforce in Silicon Valley, the high-tech companies run by Asian entrepreneurs, the mathematical skills of Russian business people, and the work ethic of Mexicans willing to take on jobs most Americans shun. The downside is that employers might use the Bush program to hold down wages unfairly. It is also another challenge to the American identity, since many immigrants share neither our language nor our cultural values. By 2050, the way things are going, the number of foreign-born people here will compose nearly half our population. Further, the Bush plan might drive up taxes, especially in California, where many immigrants of low skills and large families are supported by extensive public services.

Like it or not, Americans will have to live with the fact that while these newcomers are here illegally, they're not going to be deported. They are not fearsome aliens, just the latest iteration in an ongoing immigration drama in which, not too long ago, our parents, grandparents, and great-grandparents were the protagonists. The Bush proposal at least suggests a rational program to move us out of the impasse created by almost insoluble facts on the ground. It's not perfect, but it's a start.

 ASSIGNMENT | **Critical Review**

Do Internet or library research to find an up-to-date article in which the author presents a strong opinion on one of these controversial topics:

abortion
bilingual education
control of the Internet
globalization
grade inflation
home schooling
legalization of drugs
nuclear weapons in North Korea
prison reform
stem cell research
the U.S. blockade on Cuba
the U.S. foreign policy in the Middle East

After reading the article, print it out and write a critical review of this article. Attach a copy of the article to your paper when you hand it in.

Peer Critique

When you have completed your first draft, exchange papers (including your articles) with a classmate and evaluate your critical reviews.

Peer Critique

Evaluator   _____

Author   _____

Use this form to evaluate your classmate's critical review. Mark the document as Excellent (E), Satisfactory (S), or Unsatisfactory (U) in each of these categories:

- Grammar   correct standard English   _____
- Mechanics   correct punctuation, capitalization, spelling   _____
- Organization   logical and coherent presentation of ideas   _____
- Content   objective and clear, with specific evaluation criteria   _____
- Format   appropriate and consistent presentation on the page   _____
- Documentation   accurate and sufficient citation of sources   _____

Overall Evaluation _____

Comments

ASSIGNMENT   Critique of a Film

After watching a film of your choice, write a 500-word critique in which you summarize the plot of the movie. Then evaluate any three of these aspects: acting, script, cinematography, special effects, and musical score. In your conclusion, recommend whether others should see this film. Use this format.

I. Introduction
   A. Title of film, date of release, country of origin, director, actors
   B. Thesis: Evaluation of film

II. Summary
   A. Plot
   B. Theme

III. Evaluation
   A. Acting
   B. Script
   C. Cinematography
   D. Special Effects
   E. Musical score

IV. Conclusion
   A. Recommendation
   B. Thesis restatement

CHAPTER **10**

The Balanced Synthesis

➤ **Thesis**

➤ **Organization**

➤ **Paraphrasing**

➤ **Citation Style**

➤ **Evaluation of Internet Sources**

A synthesis is a paper that is developed from two or more sources from which the writer selects information to support a thesis. It may be organized according to various rhetorical patterns: *analysis, argument, cause-effect, chronology, classification, comparison-contrast, definition, description, enumeration, example, problem-solution,* or process. Similar to a summary, a synthesis is written in the present and present perfect tenses, except that the past tense is used for statements about specific individual past actions. Writing a synthesis requires that the writer find close relationships among the ideas found in several reading selections and combine the ideas into a cohesive, integrated whole. Moreover, the use of these sources should be balanced so that the writer does not depend on one source to the exclusion of others.

STRATEGIES

Thesis

A well-written thesis clarifies the main idea to the reader immediately, enhancing the readability of a complex document. Since the thesis is the foundation upon which a synthesis is built, it must encompass the major points that you have chosen to focus on in your paper. The thesis should be written in the present tense and may be *analytical,* an objective statement of fact, or *argumentative,* a subjective statement supporting the writer's point of view on an issue.

- **Analytical synthesis:** The writer summarizes and analyzes the ideas in the sources (articles or books) but offers no opinion on these ideas.
- **Argumentative synthesis:** The writer presents an opinion, supported by evidence from the sources (articles or books) used in the synthesis.

Discussion

With your classmates, read the thesis from each synthesis in this chapter and discuss whether it is analytical or argumentative.

"The Crisis of HIV/AIDS": Although these four articles focus on the increasing severity of the HIV/AIDS crisis, the last two present a somewhat optimistic perspective by discussing effective preventive measures that India and China have implemented.

"Health and Wealth": Although both articles suggest that this plan may be difficult to implement, giving financial aid to poor countries for health care is the morally correct action for developed countries to take.

Organization

The organization of a synthesis is an important aspect of this paper because you have to integrate information from various sources into a unified whole. Thus, outlining ideas in advance of writing is especially helpful when you are constructing a synthesis. The introduction should refer to the sources, followed by one paragraph summarizing the major conclusions of these sources. Then you can complete the essay with several paragraphs that discuss the major points supporting the thesis. On the other hand, you can briefly summarize the central ideas of the sources in the introduction and concentrate on the major points in the body of the synthesis. Each method is effective.

The two formats that follow are suggested for writing a synthesis. In the first, the writer briefly summarizes the readings in the introduction. In the second, more emphasis is given to summarizing the sources in the body of the synthesis.

Emphasis on Major Points

I. Introduction
   A. Background information about the topic
   B. Information on sources and brief summary of articles
   C. Thesis (the writer's thesis, developed from the articles)

II. Major point

III. Major point

IV. Major point

V. Conclusion
   A. Summary
   B. Restatement of thesis

Equal Emphasis on Summary and Major Points

I. Introduction
   A. Background information about the topic
   B. Information on sources
   C. Thesis (the writer's thesis, developed from the articles)

II. Summary of sources

III. Major point

IV. Major point

V. Conclusion
   A. Summary
   B. Restatement of thesis

 OUTLINE TASK

Fill in the Outline Worksheet (page 24) for "Health and Wealth" (pages 139–141).

Paraphrasing

The support for your thesis should be drawn from the outside sources that you have either been assigned or have chosen to read. This material by other writers must be paraphrased, but you can use a few short quotations. In paraphrasing, make sure that you have done a complete, not a partial, paraphrase. In a complete paraphrase, you transform the sentence structure, and you substitute synonyms for the original words without changing the meaning of the original statement. However, you should not change technical terms, such as *analog*.

Example of a complete paraphrase

Original: "A sustained, cooperative effort to improve health in developing countries would yield benefits that far exceed its costs."[1]

Paraphrase: If the developing world would work together to build better health care systems, the advantages would be much greater than the costs of these systems.

[1] Laura D'Andrea Tyson, "For Developing Countries, Health Is Wealth," *BusinessWeek*, January 14, 2002, 20.

Citation Style

As discussed in Chapter 6, The Cohesive Paragraph, writers have to distinguish between their original work and the ideas and words that belong to other writers. The method to do this is called *citation* (attribution) of sources. Attributions are given within parentheses in the text immediately after the borrowed words, phrases, and sentences or are footnoted at the bottom of a page. These sources must all be listed at the end of a document under the headings Works Cited, References, or Bibliography.

Each academic field has its own style of citation. This textbook suggests the use of the MLA style for citation, which is generally preferred for papers written in the humanities, including English and foreign languages. In MLA style, you insert the author's last name and the page number within parentheses following the quotation or paraphrase: (Lowell 258). List all your sources at the end of your paper under Works Cited, alphabetizing them by the author's last name. If no author is identified, alphabetize the sources by the first word of the title, not including *a, an,* or *the.*

Evaluation of Internet Sources

When selecting material from the Internet, you should become adept at evaluating Internet sources to determine their value and validity. With such a glut of information to choose from on the Internet, it can be difficult to find the best, most reliable material. Because there are no standards that ensure accuracy, websites vary widely in their usefulness. To determine the usefulness and quality of a website, ask these questions:

- Is the information up-to-date? Check the date when the material first appeared and when it was last updated.
- Does the author have credibility? Check the author's professional and academic qualifications.
- Is the site well known and respected? Check the reputation of the organization.
- Does the author have a bias? Check the objectivity of the writer's point of view.
- Can you trust the facts and statistics? Check the accuracy of the content by examining other sources to verify the information.

For a more detailed discussion of this subject, access the Duke University Library website, which provides an excellent explanation of how to evaluate websites: *www.lib.duke.edu/libguide/evaluating_web.htm#support/*.

EVALUATION: "THE CRISIS OF HIV/AIDS" AND "HEALTH AND WEALTH"

Read the two syntheses "The Crisis of HIV/AIDS" and "Health and Wealth," which are based on newspaper, magazine, and Internet sources. Analyze the authors' use of sources by counting the number of times each source is cited and considering whether the sources are used in a balanced way. Then evaluate the synthesis according to these criteria, and discuss your evaluation with your classmates.

Synthesis Evaluation		
Excellent +	**Satisfactory √**	**Unsatisfactory –**
• Format		_____
• Organization		_____
• Content		_____
• Understanding of topic		_____
• Style		_____
• Citation of sources		_____

Synthesis

The Crisis of HIV/AIDS

Toru Yamakami

The articles "Survey Finds China's AIDS Awareness Is Lacking; Medicine Scarce in India, Conference Is Also Told" by David Brown (*Washington Post,* July 9, 2002) and "Intelligence Study Raises Estimate of AIDS Spread" (*Washington Post,* October 1, 2002) discuss the AIDS crisis in China and India and warn that the problems will become more serious unless measures are implemented to prevent HIV/AIDS infections. These articles are based on a survey by China's State Family Planning Commission and a report by the National Intelligence Council written in 2002.

In a more recent article, "India Announces Plans to Expand AIDS Therapy Programs" (*New York Times,* November 30, 2003), the author says that India has decided to implement therapy programs for all patients with HIV/AIDS. As for China, the article "China Shift in HIV/AIDS Policy Marks Turn Around on Health" (*The Lancet,* April 24, 2004) reports that the Chinese government is beginning to change its attitude towards AIDS. These articles discuss a more proactive approach to the AIDS crisis in India and China. Henk Beckedam, the World Health Organization's China representative, reports that "Now we are starting to see them [government officials] take action" (Waldman A5). Although these four articles focus on the increasing severity of the HIV/AIDS crisis, the last two present a somewhat optimistic perspective by discussing effective preventive measures that India and China have implemented.

AIDS is a global epidemic, but many countries do not educate their citizens about it. In 2000, three-quarters of the Chinese didn't have knowledge about the cause of AIDS and ways to prevent infection. This was similar to the situation in India, where lack of education was responsible for an increase in HIV infections from 400,000 in 1990 to 4 million in 2000. In rural areas the spread of the disease was especially rapid, and nobody in the country had received antiretroviral therapy (Brown A2). According to the National Intelligence Council, not only in China and India but also in Russia, Nigeria and Ethiopia, the disease is reaching crisis proportions. There were "700,000 cases at the end of 2001 in Russia" ("Intelligence Study" A7). In Nigeria, more than 10 million cases of HIV by 2010 are predicted, and more than 7 million cases are anticipated in Ethiopia ("Intelligence Study" A7).

India has struggled to control the HIV/AIDS epidemic for many years. In response to the growing crisis, in 2003, the Indian government decided to "provide free antiretroviral therapy" to people infected with HIV/AIDS (Waldman A5). There are 4.6 million patients with HIV in the country, which is the second highest number in the world, following South Africa. However, to carry out the plan successfully, an effective health care system, a large quantity of drugs, and financial support are required (Waldman A5).

China has finally changed its attitude toward HIV/AIDS and plans to provide free tests for people with HIV in the near future. As evidence of this change, Chinese Prime minister Wen Jiabao visited an AIDS hospital and shook hands with a patient. He is the first Chinese leader to participate in such an activity (Watts 1370). This episode shows that the Chinese government has started to take measures to prevent HIV/AIDS from spreading. However, Bekedam points out that these measures are limited to central cities, and the provinces like Henan are still experiencing an increase in the number of people infected with HIV/AIDS (Watts 1370–71). In fact, the United Nations forecasts that the number of patients in China with HIV/AIDS will reach 10 million.

In the last two years, the awareness of HIV/AIDS in both India and China has been rapidly increasing. Meanwhile, there are still many critical problems that have to be solved, such as developing a budget for execution of these new plans and minimizing the differences between health care in cities and rural areas. To avoid the worst-case scenario, the governments of China and India have implemented free AIDS testing and therapy programs, and these programs will be expanded.

Works Cited

Brown, David. "Survey Finds China's AIDS Awareness Is Lacking; Medicine Scarce in India, Conference Is Also Told." *Washington Post* 9 July 2002: A2.

"Intelligence Study Raises Estimate of AIDS Spread." *Washington Post* 1 Oct. 2002: A7.

Waldman, Amy. "India Announces Plans to Expand AIDS Therapy Programs." *New York Times* 30 Nov. 2003: A5.

Watts, Jonathan. "China Shift in HIV/AIDS Policy Marks Turn Around on Health." *The Lancet* 24 April 2004: 1370–71.

Synthesis

"Health and Wealth"

MAIMOUNA ANGO

The articles "The Health of Nations" (*Economist,* December 22, 2001) and "For Developing Countries, Health Is Wealth" by Laura D'Andrea Tyson (*BusinessWeek,* January 14, 2002) address the topic of the investment by developed countries in the health care in developing countries, which would be helpful to the world economy. The articles are based on a report by the Commission on Macroeconomics & Health of the World Health Organization. Tyson, a member of the commission, explains how the investment in health will aid developing countries from an economic and humanitarian perspective and "would yield benefits that far exceed its costs" (Tyson 20). She states that if the world community is willing to invest to enhance health care services in developing countries, it will reduce disabilities and extend life, leading to higher productivity. *The Economist,* in discussing the WHO report, notes the problems that this project may encounter in its implementation by the world community. Although both articles suggest that this plan may be difficult to implement, giving financial aid to poor countries for health care is the morally correct action for developed countries to take.

According to Tyson, economists have discovered that health is closely related to economic growth. Developing nations with poor health services have less economic growth than rich countries: "Their poor health both reflects their poverty and contributes to it" (Tyson 20). Therefore, developed countries should provide financial aid to reduce poverty by promoting health care. This investment should be approximately an additional $27 billion per year above the current $6 billion per year, which is "only about 0.1% of the gross domestic product of the developed countries" (Tyson 20). The financial aid will primarily help developing countries to get drugs and fight diseases like malaria, tuberculosis and AIDS/HIV. Consequently, it "could save about 8 million lives per year by 2010" and extend life expectancy in those poor countries (Tyson 20). Each life saved will increase economic growth and productivity. In addition to this humanitarian benefit, the gain on an economic basis will be around $186 billion per year, which will be valuable for the world economy (Tyson 20).

However, *The Economist* suggests that this project may not be possible to achieve in reality. Among the obstacles, the author discusses whether the developing countries have the capacity to receive this financial investment and to utilize it properly. *The Economist* explains that poor countries "lack the domestic capacity . . . to absorb additional funding at such a rate ("The Health of Nations" 84). Furthermore, the developing countries will have to sustain this project by investing $35 billion, which might be a problem for those already deeply indebted countries. In addition, although this financial aid represents only 0.1% of the GDP of the developed countries, it is $27 billion more than current spending ("The Health of Nations" 83). Not all the developed world is willing to donate such an important amount to the developing countries. In fact, "only five donor governments meet the international target of 0.7% of GDP spent annually on official development assistance" ("The Health of Nations" 83).

Furthermore, the terrorist attacks on September 11, 2001, affected the world economy by provoking an economic downturn. One of the consequences of the global economic slowdown is that the United States is now "thinking more about al-Qaeda and anthrax than AIDS" ("The Health of Nations" 84). Economic priorities may have changed for other developed countries as well, making them less willing to spend 0.1% of their GDP to improve health services in developing countries: "Certainly the economic slowdown has made governments, and companies, look twice at assigning large sums to the war against disease" ("The Health of Nations" 84). Instead, they may prefer to spend that same amount of money on more traditional aid projects ("The Health of Nations" 83). Thus, despite the large benefits that this project may bring to the world community, the economic downturn that affected the whole world is another obstacle to its implementation.

Tyson is correct that the world community has a moral obligation to help poor nations achieve better health care. Improving health services in developing countries by donating an additional $27 billion per year by 2007 will not only be beneficial from a humanitarian view but will also help economically. It will save about 8 million lives annually and will also save $186 billion each year (Tyson 20). Unfortunately, these goals appear problematical due to a variety of reasons. Although this target represents an important opportunity for the entire world community, it is an extremely difficult goal to achieve and will require extensive international cooperation.

Works Cited

"The Health of Nations." *Economist* 22 Dec. 2001: 83–84.

Tyson, Laura D'Andrea. "For Developing Nations, Health Is Wealth." *Business-Week* 14 Jan. 2002: 20.

ASSIGNMENT Synthesis—Alternative Medicine

Write either an analytical or an argumentative synthesis that discusses the topic of alternative (complementary) medicine. The acceptance of this type of non-conventional medical treatment has grown over the years. In fact, Harvard Medical School has established the Division for Research and Education in Complementary and Integrative Medicine (*www.osher.hms.harvard.edu*), and the National Institutes of Health has established the National Center for Complementary and Alternative Medicine (*http://nccam.nih.gov*).

In your synthesis, focus on several of these forms of alternative medicine or any others in which you are interested:

    acupuncture
    aromatherapy
    biofeedback
    Chinese medical treatment
    energy healing
    folk remedies
    herbal medicine
    imagery
    massage
    naturopathy
    vegan diets
    yoga

Find relevant, recent, and reliable articles by doing Internet research. Base your synthesis on at least three articles, with equal use of information from each source. Cite your sources in the MLA in-text citation style, placing the author's last name and page number within parentheses in the text (Lowell 258). List all your sources at the end of your paper under Works Cited, alphabetizing them by the author's last name. If no author is identified, alphabetize the sources by the first word of the title, not including *a, an,* or *the.*

Peer Critique

When you have completed your first draft, exchange papers with a class-mate and evaluate your syntheses.

Peer Critique

Evaluator   _____

Author   _____

Use this form to evaluate your classmate's synthesis. Mark the document as Excellent (E), Satisfactory (S), or Unsatisfactory (U) in each of these categories:

- Grammar   correct standard English   _____
- Mechanics   correct punctuation, capitalization, spelling   _____
- Organization   logical and coherent presentation of ideas   _____
- Content   cohesive and relevant, with balanced use of sources   _____
- Format   appropriate and consistent presentation on the page   _____
- Documentation   accurate and sufficient citation of sources   _____

Overall Evaluation _____

Comments

The Persuasive Argument

An argument is a paper in which writers present their opinion on a controversial issue, justify it, and attempt to persuade readers to accept it. They express an overall point of view in the introduction and support this statement in the body of the essay with specific facts, statistics, examples, and quotations from reliable and respected sources. They must also discuss the counter-argument and show the weaknesses in it by writing a *refutation*. Similar to a summary, critical review, and synthesis, an argument is written in the present and present perfect tenses, with the exception of using the past tense for statements about specific individual past actions.

STRATEGIES

Thesis

The thesis for an argument presents an opinion that you have developed after doing extensive reading and thinking about an issue. The statement should be strongly worded and written with precision in the active voice.

Example of Theses for an Argument on Stem Cell Research

In support of embryonic stem cell research: Although embryonic stem cell research is a controversial issue involving ethical questions, researchers should continue their work because this research offers the possibility of discovering cures for serious diseases and injuries.

Against embryonic stem cell research: Although embryonic stem cell research offers the possibility of discovering cures for serious diseases and injuries, research should not continue because of the ethical issues involved.

Active and Passive Voice

Stating ideas in the active voice can be more powerful than using the passive voice. In the active voice, *someone does something*, but in the passive voice, *something is done by someone*. But choosing active or passive depends on what you want to emphasize. Although the active voice is preferred, there are cases when the passive is correct. In the examples that follow, you could use either active or passive, according to which aspect of the information you choose to emphasize in this sentence.

Active: Jonas Salk discovered the polio vaccine in 1955. (This sentence emphasizes Jonas Salk.)

Passive: The polio vaccine was discovered by Jonas Salk in 1955. (This sentence emphasizes the polio vaccine.)

✔ REVISION AND PARAGRAPH DEVELOPMENT

These sentences on the subject of stem cell research are in the passive voice.[1] Revise the sentences so that they are in the active voice. (The first sentence is a model.) After your revision, create a logically developed paragraph from these sentences by combining some sentences and adding sentence connectors if necessary. But do not change the order of the sentences. The final version of these paragraphs will argue that the U.S. government should support embryonic stem cell research. Combine the first sentence with the second sentence to create the topic sentence.

1. **Passive voice:** It is asserted by many people that stem cell research using human embryos is unethical because the right to life of the unborn is violated.

   Active voice: Many people assert that stem cell research using human embryos is unethical because it violates the right to life of the unborn.

2. In agreement with this point of view, federal funding for embryonic stem cell research was limited by George Bush on August 9, 2001, to the existing 78 lines of stem cells.

[1] The information in the exercise sentences is based on these sources: Richard Cohen, "Stem Cell Muddle," *Washington Post*, August 12, 2004, A23; Ruth R. Faden and John D. Gearhart, "Facts on Stem Cells," *Washington Post*, August 23, 2004, A15; and Rich Weiss, "The Power to Divide," *National Geographic*, July 2005, 3–27.

3. These 78 lines had been created by earlier researchers, and only about 24 are usable now.

4. Obviously, more stem cell lines are needed by government scientists working to find new treatments for spinal cord injury or cures for illnesses such as Parkinson's disease and Alzheimer's disease.

5. Only $25 million was allocated for stem cell research by the Bush administration in 2003.

6. Requests for more funding have been denied by the Bush Administration on moral grounds.

7. Early embryos are destroyed by researchers when stem cells are created.

8. This means potential human lives are being destroyed.

9. Adult stem cells are also being investigated by scientists; adult stem cells are much less likely than embryonic cells to lead to viable treatments.

10. Frequent polls have been conducted by survey research organizations to determine how Americans feel about this topic.

11. This research is supported by a majority of Americans today, according to these surveys.

12. The process of stem cell research is not understood by most people.

13. Of course, even though U.S. government scientists are limited in their study of embryonic stem cells by the Bush Administration policy, the private sector remains free to continue its work.

14. Great progress is being made in embryonic stem cell research in many countries around the world.

15. The United States has been surpassed by the U.K., China, South Korea, and Singapore, which have received strong financial support and have developed ethical guidelines for this complex area.

16. Embryonic stem cell research must be supported by the U.S. government so safe and reliable therapies can be developed as soon as possible.

Organization

The organization of an argument is the most important aspect of this type of paper. Traditionally, writers develop their arguments with two or more paragraphs supporting their thesis and one refuting (arguing against) the counter-argument. The main strategic question is whether to place the refutation after the introduction or after the supporting paragraphs. Placing your refutation after the introduction allows you to attack the opposing viewpoint immediately, which can have a great impact on the reader as he or she reads through the remainder of your argument. On the other hand, placing your refutation right before the conclusion can be an emphatic way to lead to the restatement of your thesis.

In the body paragraphs, you face a similar issue of strategy: whether to discuss the strongest point first (descending order) or last (ascending order). Generally, descending order is best when one major point is stronger than the other points.

This format can be used for writing an argument.

Refutation Last

I. Introduction
   A. Background information about the topic
   B. Thesis (the writer's opinion)

II. Support for argument

III. Support for argument

IV. Refutation of counter-argument

V. Conclusion
   A. Summary
   B. Restatement of thesis

Refutation First

I. Introduction
   A. Background information about the topic
   B. Thesis (the writer's opinion)

II. Refutation of counter-argument

III. Support for argument

IV. Support for argument

V. Conclusion
   A. Summary
   B. Restatement of thesis

Persuasive Tone

The key to writing a successful argument is presenting your thesis and major points in a logically persuasive tone that is supported by well-chosen evidence.

Evidence

Techniques of persuasion include the use of current evidence (facts and statistics), the previously accepted data that support your point of view, and the testimony of recognized experts. Be sure to cite your sources when you make use of this information. When choosing the points that justify your position, ask these questions:

- Is the information up-to-date and accurate?
- Are my sources for quotations recognized experts in this field?
- Have I selected the most convincing information?
- Have I fully explained the points that justify my position?

Advocacy

By presenting strong evidence, selecting concrete nouns and strong verbs, and preferring active to passive voice, you can create a persuasive tone. But something more is required to construct a superior document: You have to be an advocate for your point of view, as the British scientist Richard Dawkins writes in the Preface to his book *The Blind Watchmaker: Why the Evidence of Evolution Reveals a Universe without Design:*

> Explaining is a difficult art. You can explain something so that your reader understands the words, and you can explain something so that the reader feels it in the marrow of his bones. To do the latter, it sometimes isn't enough to lay the evidence before the reader in a dispassionate way. You have to become an advocate and use the tricks of the advocate's trade. This book is not a dispassionate scientific treatise. Other books on Darwinism are, and many of them are intelligent and informative and should be read in conjunction with this one. Far from being dispassionate, it has to be confessed that in parts this book is written with a passion which, in a professional scientific journal, might excite comment. Certainly it seeks to inform, but it also seeks to persuade and even—one can specify *aims* without presumption—to inspire.[2]

Interpretation and Paraphrase: *The Blind Watchmaker*

In 1859 Charles Darwin published *On the Origin of Species*, a book that presented his theory of evolution, natural selection. According to this theory, life forms change through time, and environmental conditions (nature) determine the survival and reproduction of an organism. Organisms with more adaptive traits will live, and those with less adaptive traits will die out. While Darwin's theory of evolution is generally accepted today, there are those who do not agree with it.

Read aloud the short excerpt by Richard Dawkins, which is the final paragraph in his book *The Blind Watchmaker: Why the Evidence of Evolution Reveals a Universe without Design*. As a class, discuss the nouns, verbs, adjectives, and adverbs in the excerpt, and work together to interpret the meaning of the excerpt. Then write a paraphrase of these two sentences. Compare your paraphrase to the original sentences in terms of being persuasive. Remember that when you paraphrase, you should not change technical terms such as *evolution theory* and *natural selection*.

---

[2] Richard Dawkins, *The Blind Watchmaker: Why the Evidence of Evolution Reveals a Universe without Design* (New York and London: W. W. Norton, 1996), xiv.

If there are versions of the evolution theory that deny slow gradualism, and deny the central role of natural selection, they may be true in particular cases.[3] But they cannot be the whole truth, for they deny the very heart of the evolution theory, which gives it the power to dissolve astronomical improbabilities and explain prodigies of apparent miracle.[4]

Paraphrase . . . .

_____

_____

_____

_____

_____

_____

Refutation of Counter-Argument

In a refutation, you describe the major arguments of your opponents, and then explain why these arguments are inaccurate, unsupported by evidence, misleading, or based on false assumptions. Be clear, precise, and definite in your refutation of these counter arguments.

Analysis of a Refutation: "Embryonic Stem Cell Research"

The writer of this paragraph, using a formal academic style, includes quotations from experts to refute the most common arguments against cell research. Identify the two main arguments the author uses in this refutation.

---

[3] *Slow gradualism* and *natural selection* are parts of Darwin's theory of evolution, which argues that evolutionary changes occur very gradually and are determined by nature.

[4] Dawkins, *The Blind Watchmaker*, 318.

Embryonic Stem Cell Research

Some members of religious groups argue against stem cell research using human embryos because they believe that life begins at the moment of conception. Thus, they "abhor the destruction of embryos . . . and object to techniques in which embryos are cloned for the harvesting of stem cells" (Weintraub 104). Moreover, they believe researchers are taking control of the life and death processes, a power that, in their eyes, only God should have. This reasoning is based on faulty assumptions and lacks logic. According to scientists, a human embryo, although created when sperm and egg merge, is not viable until at least twelve weeks. Stem cell research uses a three-to-five-day-old embryo. "It has no consciousness, no self-awareness, no ability to feel love or pain" (Kinsley 88). This means that the early embryos cannot be considered human beings with human rights. Furthermore, scientists have been studying the complex causes of illness through their experiments and have made great discoveries, such as heart transplants for people with heart disease and in-vitro fertilization to help infertile couples have children. Since stem cell research may be a critical phase in finding cures and treatments for major diseases and injuries, scientists must not be prevented from continuing their groundbreaking work.

Works Cited

Kinsley, Michael. "The False Controvery of Stem Cells." *Time* 31 May 2004: 88.

Weintraub, Arlene. "Biotech Frontier: Repairing the Engines of Life." *BusinessWeek* 24 May 2004: 104.

Analysis of a Refutation: The Inheritance of Genes

Let us now read a less traditional refutation paragraph from *River Out of Eden* by Richard Dawkins, who argues against the common misconception that genes improve with each generation. He writes in an informal, conversational style, using a metaphor to explain why good genes, not bad genes, are passed on unchanged through the centuries. Identify the metaphor and explain its meaning.

It is tempting to think that when ancestors did successful things, the genes they passed on to their children were, as a result, upgraded relative to the genes they had received from their parents. Something about their success rubbed off on their genes, and that is why their descendants are so good at flying, swimming, courting. Wrong, utterly wrong! Genes do not improve in the using; they are just passed on, unchanged except for very rare random errors. It is not success that makes good genes. It is good genes that make success, and nothing an individual does during its lifetime has any effect whatever upon its genes. Those individuals born with good genes are the most likely to grow up to become successful ancestors; therefore good genes are more likely than bad to get passed on to the future. Each generation is a filter, a sieve: good genes tend to fall through the sieve into the next generation; bad genes tend to end up in bodies that die young or without reproducing. Bad genes may pass through the sieve for a generation or two, perhaps because they have the luck to share a body with good genes. But you need more than luck to navigate successfully through a thousand sieves in succession, one sieve under the other. After a thousand successive generations, the genes that have made it through are likely to be the good ones.[5]

[5] Richard Dawkins, *River Out of Eden: A Darwinian View of Life* (New York: HarperCollins, Inc., 1995), 2–3.

EVALUATION: "PRESERVING THE VALLEGRANDE ROCK ART SITES IN BOLIVIA"

Read the paper on the Vallegrande Rock Art Sites in Bolivia (pages 155–57), which is based on two Internet sources. Complete these tasks, and then evaluate the argument with your classmates.

- Put brackets around the thesis (main idea) of the argument.
- Underline the topic sentence in each paragraph.
- Put brackets around the supporting facts, statistics, examples, and quotations in each paragraph.
- Underline the closing sentence in each paragraph.
- Highlight all the adjectives and adverbs.
- Identify the refutation paragraph.

	Argument Evaluation	
Excellent +	**Satisfactory √**	**Unsatisfactory –**
• Format		_____
• Organization		_____
• Content		_____
• Understanding of topic		_____
• Style		_____
• Refutation		_____
• Citation of Sources		_____

Argument

Preserving the Vallegrande Rock Art Sites in Bolivia

Claudia Ordinez

Bolivia has a diversity of cultural and historical sites such as the Vallegrande Rock Art Sites, which contain paintings on rocks, called petroglyphs, dating from centuries ago. The World Monuments Fund, a private organization in New York that "seeks to focus public attention on sites in crisis through its World Monuments Watch program," publishes a biannual list of the 100 Most Endangered Sites *(www.wmf.org)*. The Vallegrande Rock Art Sites appeared for the first time on the 2004 list. They are one of the most important cultural treasures in Bolivia because they have a great variety of colorful paintings and engravings that were created over thousands of years; therefore, the Bolivian government should immediately develop a plan to preserve and protect these endangered sites.

The Vallegrande Rock Art Sites, which are located in an area west of Santa Cruz, are uniquely beautiful and attract many Bolivians. However, they are threatened by uncontrolled tourism and vandalism. "With their extraordinary paintings and petroglyphs dating from possibly 6000 B.C. to 1950 A.D., the Andean rock art sites El Buey, Toro Muerto, Palmarito, and Paja Colorada are among the most significant of their kind in Bolivia. Palmarito is still revered as a place of pilgrimage by the local community" *(www.wmf.org)*. El Buey and Palmarito have not yet been damaged, but vandals have looted and harmed both Toro Muerto and Paja Colorada. Although the local governments are in favor of allowing tourists to visit these sites in supervised programs, no proposals for their preservation or protection have been developed and no organized tourism programs have been implemented *(www.wmf.org)*.

Serious investigation of these sites in Bolivia is just now beginning, so many regions have not been explored, and there is no exact chronology of when the rocks were painted (Bolivian Rock Art Research Society). According to the World Monuments Watch, "the sites are in desperate need of a professional survey, educational campaign, and training program, as well as security precautions and visitor services" *(www.wmf.org)*. Because of limited government funding for research, a private scientific institution, Sociedad de Investigacion del Arte Rupestre de Bolivia (SIARB), supported by the Bradshaw Foundation in Geneva and the embassies of Germany and the Netherlands, has registered, recorded, and published information on the rock art sites. "Surveys of rock art regions by SIARB have already registered approximately 1,000 rock art sites all over Bolivia, though mainly in the highlands and valleys" (Bolivian Rock Art Research Society). The SIARB has begun working with the municipality of Vallegrande to address the problem of preserving these sites, but it lacks the resources to complete a project of this size.

Some people in Bolivia question the wisdom of allocating funding to the rock art sites because of the fact that Bolivia is a poor country with a large part of its population living in extreme poverty without the basic necessities of food and shelter. They believe any available money should go to helping those in the lower economic strata, not to preserving ancient archeological sites. Also, objections have been raised about whether promoting tourism would damage the rock art, some of which is already in a fragile condition, and increase vandalism. Another concern is that trying to repair and preserve these sites might not be the appropriate way to treat such ancient treasures, which, many believe, should be left untouched in their original condition. However, because of their great historic and artistic value, the Bolivian government could get funding from wealthy individuals or international institutions for these rock art sites. It could then hire experienced archeologists and conservationists who would know how to conserve these cultural treasures and protect them from vandalism. Finally, well-organized tourism could be a welcome source of income for Bolivia. Thus, these concerns are misplaced and reveal a misunderstanding of the purpose and benefits of historic preservation.

It is tremendously important for the Bolivian government to plan a strategy for preservation of this rich archeological heritage. Even though the SIARB is making progress on this issue, it has not yet completed a study to establish the chronology of all the rock art paintings in Bolivia. Furthermore, many Bolivians are not aware of the true value of these sites. Thus, tourism specialists and archeologists should develop an educational campaign to emphasize the need to preserve these sites and also to promote and regulate tourism, which could benefit the weak Bolivian economy. Finally, the government must provide financial support for the study of the Vallegrande Rock Art Sites, which are a priceless part of Bolivia's historical and cultural heritage.

Works Cited

"Bolivian Rock Art Research Society (SIARB)." Bradshaw Foundation. <http://www.bradshawfoundation.com/Bolivia/main/html/>.

"Vallegrande Area Rock Art Sites: Vallegrande and Saipina, Bolivia." World Monuments Fund. World Monuments Watch 2004: List of 100 Most Endangered Sites. <http://www. wmf.org/>.

ASSIGNMENT | **Argument—The World Monuments Fund**

Many ancient monuments and historic cultural sites around the world are in danger of being damaged or destroyed. For example, the Pyramids in Egypt and Machu Picchu, an Incan ruin in Peru, have suffered damage as a result of extensive tourism and air pollution.

Access the website for the World Monuments Fund at *www.wmf.org/*. This private organization works to protect historical art and architecture through its World Monuments Watch program and its biannual list of the 100 Most Endangered Sites. After you read the information on the most endangered sites, choose an endangered site to investigate as the subject of an argument.

Guidelines for Argument
- Find at least two articles from the Internet that discuss this cultural or historic site, and write an argument based on these articles.
- Cite your sources in the MLA in-text citation format, placing the author's last name and the page number within parentheses after the information you have quoted or paraphrased. If no author is identified, use the title.
- List the sources in alphabetical order at the end of the paper as Works Cited.
- Include a photograph of the site with your paper if you can locate one.
- Develop a thesis that presents an argument, such as this one:

    The Basra Ancient City in Syria, which is an endangered site, should be preserved because it is a valuable example of traditional Syrian architecture.

| ASSIGNMENT | Argument—"Constitutional Topic: Official Language" |

Read the article titled "Constitutional Topic: Official Language," from the U.S. Constitution Online. This website lists other sites concerning Official English in the United States. Access these sites as well as the sites concerning the official languages of other countries. After reading about this topic, choose to argue either for or against making English the official language of the United States.

Cite your sources in the MLA in-text citation style, placing the author's last name and page number within parentheses in the text: (Lowell 258). List all your sources at the end of your paper under Works Cited, alphabetizing them by the author's last name. If no author is identified, alphabetize the sources by the first word of the title, not including *a*, *an*, or *the*.

Constitutional Topic: Official Language[6]

Many people are surprised to learn that the United States has no official language. As one of the major centers of commerce and trade, and a major English-speaking country, many assume that English is the country's official language. But despite efforts over the years, the United States has no official language.

Almost every session of Congress, an amendment to the Constitution is proposed in Congress to adopt English as the official language of the United States. Other efforts have attempted to take the easier route of changing the U.S. Code to make English the official language. As of this writing, the efforts have not been successful.

Here is the text of a proposed amendment. This particular bill was introduced in the House of Representatives as H.J. Res. 16 (107th Congress):

---

[6] The U.S. Constitution Online, "Constitutional Topic, Official Language," *www.usconstitution. net/consttop_lang.html.*

The English language shall be the official language of the United States. As the official language, the English language shall be used for all public acts including every order, resolution, vote, or election, and for all records and judicial proceedings of the Government of the United States and the governments of the several States.

Also introduced in the 107th Congress was this text from H.R. 3333:

The Government of the United States shall preserve and enhance the role of English as the official language of the United States of America. Unless specifically stated in applicable law, no person has a right, entitlement, or claim to have the Government of the United States or any of its officials or representatives act, communicate, perform or provide services, or provide materials in any language other than English. If exceptions are made, that does not create a legal entitlement to additional services in that language or any language other than English.

Often these bills are in response to legislation recognizing non-English languages in public discourse of some kind. H.R. 3333, for example, also explicitly repealed the Bilingual Education Act, which authorized funds to educate American students in their native tongue as well as to provide specialized training in the learning of English.

The most recent efforts to promote English as the official language has come as more and more immigration from Spanish-speaking and Eastern nations (such as China and Vietnam) has brought an influx of non–English speakers to the United States. According to the 1990 Census, 13.8 percent of U.S. residents speak some non–English language at home. 2.9 percent, or 6.7 million people, did not speak English at all, or could not speak it well.

The ACLU, which is part of a group opposed to establishing a national official language, has published a paper detailing reasons that such a move should be opposed. It starts by mentioning an effort by John Adams, in 1780, to establish an official academy devoted to English, a move which was rejected at the time as undemocratic. The ACLU notes past efforts at English-only laws that abridged the rights of non–English speakers or which generally made life difficult for large non–English speaking populations. One example cited in Dade County, Florida, where, after a 1980 English-only law was passed, Spanish signs on public transportation were removed.

The ACLU believes that English-only laws can violate the U.S. Constitution's protection of due process (especially in courts where no translation service would be offered) and equal protection (for example, where English-only ballots would be used where bilingual ones were available in the past).

English-only proponents like U.S. English counter that English-only laws generally have exceptions for public safety and health needs. They note that English-only laws help governments save money by allowing publication of official documents in a single language, saving on translation and printing costs, and that English-only laws promote the learning of English by non-English speakers. One example offered is that of Canada, with two official languages, English and French. The Canadian government itself has addressed this issue, noting that in 1996–7, only $260 million Canadian dollars were spent on bilingual services.

There has been at least one interesting contrast to the pro-English efforts. In 1923, Illinois officially declared that English would no longer be the official language of Illinois—but American would be. Many of Illinois' statutes refer to "the American language," (example: 225 ILCS 705/27.01) though the official language of the state is now English (5 ILCS 460/20).

According to U.S. English, the following states have existing official language laws on their books: Alabama, Alaska, Arkansas, California, Colorado, Florida, Georgia, Hawaii, Illinois, Indiana, Iowa, Kentucky, Louisiana, Massachusetts, Mississippi, Missouri, Montana, Nebraska, New Hampshire, North Carolina, North Dakota, South Carolina, South Dakota, Tennessee, Utah, Virginia, Wyoming. A small handful date back more than a few decades, such as Louisiana (1811) and Nebraska (1920), but most official language statutes have been passed since the 1970s.

Peer Critique

When you have completed your first draft, exchange papers with a class-mate and evaluate your arguments.

Peer Critique

Evaluator   _____

Author   _____

Use this form to evaluate your classmate's summary. Mark the document as Excellent (E), Satisfactory (S), or Unsatisfactory (U) in each of the following categories:

- Grammar   correct standard English   _____
- Mechanics   correct punctuation, capitalization, spelling   _____
- Organization   logical and coherent presentation of ideas   _____
- Content   persuasive and relevant, with effective refutation   _____
- Format   appropriate and consistent presentation on the page   _____
- Documentation   accurate and sufficient citation of sources   _____

Overall Evaluation _____

Comments

The Scholarly Research Paper

A research paper is a lengthy document that uses numerous sources to answer a question or analyze an issue. The topic of writing a research paper is complex enough to be a book in itself, but this chapter provides the basic information necessary for undergraduate students to succeed in this task. Although there are many kinds of research papers, we will discuss the general academic research paper assigned in liberal arts courses, not the standard empirical research paper.[1]

Writing a research paper is an act of scholarship. The writer engages in an in-depth investigation of a meaningful topic, synthesizing information from a variety of sources to support and prove a thesis. The best research papers show originality of thought, offering new perspectives on a subject. Most research papers are analytical, studying the causes and effects of historical events or the solutions to contemporary problems. Documentation is essential since the paper is built on research; sources must be cited for all information, both quoted and paraphrased, used in the paper.

The style of a research paper is formal and objective, and the tone is impersonal although it may become personal when the paper involves an interpretation of a work of art or literature. Similar to a synthesis, a research paper is usually written in the present and present perfect tenses, but tense usage can be complex and varied in such a long paper. For instance, writers should use the past and past perfect tenses for statements about past actions: *Home schooling in the United States **was legalized** in 1993.* Also, when writers refer to a specific research study in the past, they use the past tense: *Talbot **found** that home-schooled children **performed** better on achievement tests than children in public schools.*

Research papers require a wide range of tasks and skills: critical thinking, reading, writing, analysis, synthesis, research, graphic design, and technology. The process of constructing this type of paper can be challenging but also rewarding. The key is for the writer to manage the process with flexibility, being ready to make revisions in accord with his or her ongoing research, while maintaining focus on the underlying goal: a well-documented, accurate, and readable paper.

---

[1] See John M. Swales and Christine B. Feak, *Academic Writing for Graduate Students, 2ᵈ ed.* (Ann Arbor: The University of Michigan Press, 2004), for an explanation of this type of paper, which is written in the Introduction, Methods, Results, Discussion (IMRD) format.

STRATEGIES

Step 1: Topic Choice

The beginning of this process, the pre-writing stage, is in some ways the most important aspect of a research project since the first step in writing a research paper is *selecting a topic*. Ideally, you are truly interested in your topic and, if possible, already have background knowledge about it. But myriad factors influence the topic choice: requirements of the assignment, including number of sources and pages; goal of the paper (analytical or argumentative); and depth of research anticipated. Thus, you should not make this decision quickly.

In order to produce a research paper, you have to read a variety of sources, both online and hard copy. Depending on the assignment's purpose and goal, the number of required sources could range from 5 to 25 and could include popular publications like *Time* magazine or scholarly publications like *Foreign Affairs*. Therefore, one major criterion for selecting a topic is the number of reliable sources that you have access to and can understand with your present level of knowledge.

A second criterion is the inherent value of the subject. Will educating yourself on this subject be a worthwhile expenditure of your time and energy? Will the analysis in your paper be original in approach and useful to others or just a repeat performance of a common topic like capital punishment? Excellent general subject areas include historical events, economic or political developments in a country, changes in social or cultural attitudes, the achievements of great men or women, the major effects of globalization, scientific advances, and the impact of information technology. Of course, all these general subject areas have to be narrowed down to a specific aspect of the subject.

Step 2: Preliminary Research

- **Computer Search:** Choose one of the general subjects listed on page 166. Then do a computer search to determine the number of potential sources that you would have access to if you wrote a research paper on this topic. In your search, include newspaper and magazine articles, books, and websites. (See Appendix F, Internet Research.) Use the Preliminary Research Form on page 167.

- **Research Question:** After a brief review of the available information, read several articles on the general topic you have selected. Then *develop a research question* that will focus your attention on one precise aspect of the topic. This question generally begins with a *wh* word *(who, what, when, where, why)* and will probably change during the course of your research, but it is an excellent way to begin the research process.

   Example of a Research Question: What are the disadvantages of the home-schooling system in comparison with the public school system in the United States?

General Subjects
Argentina's Eva Peron
Albert Einstein's Theories
The Basque Separatist Movement in Spain
The Caste System in India
The Cultural Traditions of Japanese Families
The Decline of the Soviet Union
Gene Therapy
The History of the Olympics
Home Schooling in the United States
Impressionist Art
Language Acquisition in Children
The Lewis and Clark Expedition
Machu Picchu in Peru
Marie Curie's Scientific Work
Petra in Jordan
The Political History of Hong Kong
The Science of Nanotechnology
Saudi Arabia's Economic Development
Stonehenge in England
Wilbur and Orville Wright
Wireless Technology

PRELIMINARY RESEARCH FORM

After narrowing your topic by doing a computer search and writing a research question for your specific topic, fill out the preliminary research form.

General Subject Area _____

Specific Topic of Investigation _____

Research Question _____

_____

Preliminary Sources (Identify three sources for each category.)
- Articles (author, title, source, date, pages)

_____

_____

_____

- Books (author, title, publisher, location of publisher, date of publication)

_____

_____

_____

- Internet (URL address and title of website)

_____

_____

_____

Write one paragraph explaining why you are interested in this topic.

_____

_____

_____

_____

_____

Step 3: Bibliography—Evaluating Sources

Because of the Internet, today's writer can do research more easily than writers in the past. We have innumerable resources from which to assemble a bibliography for a research paper. An immense (and chaotic) global library is at our fingertips. The challenge is to use this resource wisely and efficiently. Since there are no standards or rules that apply to what is published on the Internet, anyone can publish anything. This makes it essential to be able to *evaluate Internet sources for their reliability, currency, and usefulness*, as discussed in Chapter 10, The Balanced Synthesis. When deciding on which sources to use, consider these factors:

- Is the information up-to-date? Check the date when the material first appeared and when it was last updated.
- Does the author have credibility? Check the author's professional and academic qualifications.
- Does the author have a bias? Check the objectivity of the writer's point of view.
- Is the site well known and respected? Check the reputation of the sponsoring organization.
- Can you trust the facts and statistics? Check the accuracy of the content by examining other sources to verify the information.

For a more detailed discussion of this subject, access the Duke University Library Website, which provides an excellent explanation of how to evaluate websites: *www.lib.duke.edu/libguide/evaluating_web.htm#support/*.

In most cases, a bibliography should not be composed of purely Internet sources. It should also contain books, journals, magazines, and newspapers that are not published online. When selecting these sources, consider the date of publication, the credibility and objectivity of the author, and the reliability of the facts and statistics.

Step 4: Hypothesis and Thesis

Having done preliminary research, evaluated and selected your sources, and read and taken notes on some material, you are prepared for the next logical step: *constructing a hypothesis*. Your hypothesis is a one- or two-sentence statement of the issue you are investigating for your research paper. After you have completed your reading and research, you will rewrite your hypothesis as a thesis. In other words, your **hypothesis** is your understanding of or prediction about the issue *before* you have done research and reading. Your **thesis** reflects what you have discovered *after* your research and reading. It is the controlling idea of your document; therefore, it must be supported and proven in the body of your paper through the incorporation of quotations and paraphrases of credible sources that you have discovered through your research.

> **Example of a Hypothesis:** Microsoft Corporation is a monopoly that should be broken up because it has limited competition in the software industry.

> **Example of a Thesis:** Although Microsoft Corporation is a huge and powerful corporation, it is not a monopoly and should not be broken up.

A research paper is actually an extended synthesis in which the writer synthesizes information from various sources in order to support a thesis. As discussed in Chapter 10, The Balanced Synthesis, the thesis for a research paper can be either analytical or argumentative, depending on the purpose of the paper.

> **Analytical thesis:** The results of extensive research reveal that home schooling is becoming an increasingly popular form of education in the United States.

> **Argumentative thesis:** Home schooling should be encouraged because students who are home schooled excel academically on achievement tests and exhibit stronger social skills than students who are educated in public schools.

 **ASSIGNMENT**   Developing a Hypothesis

Write a hypothesis for the specific topic of investigation you selected for the preliminary research form on page 167. Share your hypothesis with your classmates.

_____

_____

_____

_____

Step 5: Research Proposal

If you have continued to search for new sources and read material on your topic, you are ready to construct a research proposal outline that presents the preliminary thesis, major points, and topic sentences of your paper. You should also include the sources that you anticipate using, indicating the sections of your paper in which you plan to incorporate them. Of course, this outline does not represent the final form of your paper; it is only a proposal that may undergo major revisions. But having an outline to guide you will facilitate the writing process and help you to manage the various tasks involved in such a complex project.

Model Research Proposal

Home Schooling in the United States

KARINE HEULLUY

I. Introduction
   A. Background
      Home schooling offers an individualized approach to learning that allows parents to adapt a curriculum that meets their educational goals for their children. Since home schooling was legalized in 1993, it has been rapidly gaining in popularity as an alternative to public schooling in the United States.
   B. Thesis: Although home schooling in the United States has led to high performance on achievement tests and excellent social skills, the program would benefit from cooperation with U.S. public school administrators.
   C. Source: Williamson, Kerri Bennet. *Home Schooling: Answering Questions.* Springfield, MA: C. C. Thomas, 1989.

II. Body
   A. Major point: Description of Home-Schooling Families
   B. Topic sentence: Home-schooled children usually come from large, highly educated, white, two-parent families who want a better education for their children and are often Christians.

   C. Sources:
      Gewertz, Catherine. "Study Estimates 850,000 U.S. Children Schooled at Home." *Education Week*, 8 Aug. 2001: 12.
      Guterson, David. *Family Matters: Why Home Schooling Makes Sense*. New York: Harcourt Brace Jovanovich, 1992.

III. Body
   A. Major point: Criticism of Home Schooling
   B. Topic sentence: Critics believe that home schooling can be dangerous if the purpose is to narrow the students' educational experience for political, social, or religious purposes.
   C. Source: Cloud, John, and Jodie Morse. "Home Sweet School." *Time* 27 Aug. 2001: 46–54.

IV. Body
   A. Major point: Better Test Performance
   B. Topic sentence: The data show that home-schooled children perform better on achievement tests than children who attend public schools.
   C. Source: Talbot, Margaret. "The New Counterculture." *The Atlantic* Nov. 2001: 136–43.

 V. Body
   A. Major point: Excellent Socialization
   B. Topic sentence: The data show that home-schooled children are more mature and socially adept than public-schooled children because they are not segregated in classes by age.
   C. Sources:
      Learn in Freedom: *http://learninfreedom.org*
      Meighan, Roland. *The Next Learning System and Why Home Schoolers Are Trailblazers*. Nottingham, England: Educational Heretics Press, 1997.

VI. Body
   A. Major point: Adversarial Attitude between Home Schooling and Public Schools
   B. Topic sentence: An adversarial attitude exists between home-schooling advocates and public school administrators because public school administrators see home schooling as a challenge to their system.
   C. Source: Mayberry, Maralee. *Home Schooling: Parents as Educators*. Thousands Oaks: Corwin Press, 1995.

VII. Conclusion
    A. Major point: Changes in Attitudes and Cooperation
    B. Topic sentence: Although home schooling in the United States has led to excellent test performance and social skills, home-schooling advocates and public school administrators should cooperate and exchange ideas in order to improve the academic and social environment of the home schooling system.
    C. Source: Romanowski, Michael H. "Undoing the 'Us vs. Them' of Public and Home Schooling." *The Education Digest* May 2001: 41–45.

Outlining a Research Proposal

Review the model research proposal on pages 170 and 171. Then complete the research proposal outline with the information you have gathered on the topic you selected on page 166. Write your preliminary thesis statement as you see it at this point, with the knowledge that you may revise it after you complete your research.

Research Proposal Title

  I. Introduction
    A. Background
    B. Thesis
    C. Sources

  II. Body
    A. Major point
    B. Topic sentence
    C. Sources

  III. Body
    A. Major point
    B. Topic sentence
    C. Sources

  IV. Body
    A. Major point
    B. Topic sentence
    C. Sources

   V. Body
       A. Major point
       B. Topic sentence
       C. Sources

  VI. Conclusion
       A. Summary
       B. Thesis restatement
       C. Sources

Step 6: Writing the Paper

Incorporation of Sources

The challenge of writing an effective research paper lies in being able to integrate your own ideas and opinions with the information you have taken from your sources. This is a skill that improves with practice, but it is not something that everyone can do easily. The interweaving of quotations and paraphrases with your commentary should be logical and smooth. The use of phrases that introduce quotations, such as *according to Chapman, as Chapman states in his article*, and *in Chapman's words*, can help fuse these two different types of information into a unified and cohesive whole.

Although you have to support your thesis and justify your conclusions with information from your sources, quotations and paraphrases should not make up the entire paper. Your role is to construct a context for the quoted and paraphrased material by writing statements of introduction, explanation, interpretation, inference, and summary. Thus, the author of a research paper has to carefully balance the material in the paper, without going to the extremes of using too many quotations or not incorporating enough quotations.

✓ INCORPORATING SOURCES

Read the quotations from the reference *The Elements of Style* by William Strunk and E. B. White.[2] Then write two paragraphs about your ability to write well in the English language. Incorporate several of the quotations or paraphrases of the quotations into the paragraphs so that you achieve a balance between your ideas and the quotations. The following two intoductory sentences should begin your paragraph.

In *The Elements of Style,* William Strunk and E. B. White present their guidelines for writing well, which include rules of grammar, principles of composition, and an approach to style. Since I want to write well in English, I have been studying these aspects and have improved my writing.

"In general, however, it is nouns and verbs, not their assistants, that give to good writing its toughness and color."

"Revising is part of writing. Few writers are so expert that they can produce what they are after on the first try."

"Rich, ornate prose is hard to digest, generally unwholesome, and sometimes nauseating."

"The language is perpetually in flux: it is a living stream, shifting, changing, receiving new strength from a thousand tributaries, losing old forms in the backwaters of time."

"Writing good standard English is no cinch, and before you have managed it you will have encountered enough rough country to satisfy even the most adventurous spirit."

"Style takes its final shape more from attitudes of mind than from principles of composition, for, as an elderly practitioner once remarked, 'Writing is an act of faith, not a trick of grammar.'"

"If one is to write, one must believe—in the truth and worth of the scrawl, in the ability of the reader to receive and decode the message."

[2] William Strunk, Jr., and E. B. White, *The Elements of Style, 4th ed.* (New York: Longman, 2000), 72, 85.

Writing Well in English

_____

_____

_____

_____

_____

_____

_____

_____

_____

_____

_____

_____

_____

_____

_____

_____

_____

_____

_____

The Introduction

In many ways, the introduction is the most difficult section of a research paper to write. In fact, some writers prefer writing the introduction after they have completed the rest of the paper and know exactly how they want to introduce their topic. The purposes of an introduction are to establish a background and context for the topic of the paper, to state the thesis, and to attract the interest of the reader. Ideas should be developed using general to specific organization, placing the thesis at the end of the introduction. In long papers, an introduction may be four or five paragraphs. Each succeeding paragraph increases in specificity, leading to the thesis statement.

The introduction also establishes the style of the research paper, which is generally objective and formal. Most writers avoid the use of first-person pronouns, contractions, idioms, and dramatic language, preferring an analytical, impersonal, factual tone. Of course, there are exceptions to this. For example, writers may include a personal thesis statement, such as *In this paper I will analyze . . .* or *My purpose in this research paper is to. . . .* However, these statements are not as effective as an objective, impersonal thesis statement.

Example of Thesis: Turkey should become a member of the EU in order to refute images of a "clash of civilizations" and to prevent the security threat from fundamentalist Muslim states.

The Abstract

An abstract, which is a short summary (usually between 50 and 200 words) of a longer document, is the first page of a research paper or formal report although it is written last. A **descriptive** abstract presents the topics covered in the document but offers no conclusions; it is similar to a table of contents. An **informative** abstract provides the reader with the thesis, major points, findings, and conclusions of the document. Abstracts are written in a formal, objective, and concise style. Technical language may be used if appropriate to the topic of the paper.

PROOFREADING AND EDITING: SUDAN

Read the informative abstract written for a 15-page research paper on Sudan, and proofread it to identify and correct errors in grammar, punctuation, and spelling. Then edit it for clarity, coherence, conciseness, and precision. In your revision reduce the number of words from 271 to about 200.

Abstract

Sudan

Since it's independence in 1956, Sudan has been ruled by a series of coalition and military regimes, however neither type were able to put an end to the disasterous civil war and local rebellions. In 1989 the National Islamic Front (NIF) has gained control of the government. Currently, millions of refugees are starving in Darfur because the brutality of this government. To put down a military uprising, the NIF destroyed the peoples means of agricultural production, that is a form of genocide.[3]

Political turmoil has for so long characterized the country. Indeed, as the political events overshadow the economy, economic and social development are rare. Following independence, Sudan embarked on a series of development plans that were oriented towards broadening the economic structure and expanding export. Unfortunately, due to political instability, economic mismanagement, enviromental problems civil war, and liquidity problems,

---

[3] Eric Reeves, "Regime Change in Sudan," *Washington Post*, August 23, 2004, A15.

most development plans did not run their full lives; hence, they failed to acheive their goals.

Today, Sudan exemplifies every problem suffered by Africa, and the other developing nations. Environmental problems, civil war, poverty, diseases, as well as famine. In addition, today, the country is trapped into a sever economic malaise that threatens its sovereignty: huge external debt and skyrocketing deficit. The worsening financial situation in Sudan helped to pave the way for multilateral institutions—the World Bank and the International Monetary Fund (IMF)—to impose their paradigms of development. In addition, the Bank and the IMF appear not to have learnt from their past experience, and continued to dictate the same structural adjustment programs and growth models that derived peasants off the land and led them to rebel.

Outline and Evaluation: "Turkey's Integration into the European Union (EU)"

After reading the research paper "Turkey's Integration into the European Union (EU)," fill in the sentence outline of the paper on page 194. Then evaluate it with your classmates using the Research Paper Evaluation form on page 196. Note the format of the title page, which includes the title, author, course number, instructor, and date.

Turkey's Integration
into the European Union (EU)

Anna Schily
ELI 201.002
Professor Shulman
April 12, 2005

Abstract

In the past half century, Turkey has tried to become a member of the "exclusive club" of European nations, the European Union (EU). The accession process started in 1964 but was never completed. This delay in full integration might stem from fundamental differences in culture and religion or from European discontent with the instability of the Turkish government. Despite these reservations and obstacles, Turkey's membership in the EU is vital in order to build a secure and culturally diverse Europe.

Historically speaking, Turkey is more closely connected to the EU than other current candidates; it is a member of intergovernmental European institutions and a founding member of NATO. Culturally, however, Turkey has been marginalized as a Muslim nation. In fact, an alliance with Turkey would strengthen European security. In the fight against terrorism, Turkey would serve as a connection to the Islamic world.

Although Turkey is a secular democratic state, it has not achieved full democratization. Thus, the government has undertaken political and economic reforms required by the EU in regard to human rights and treatment of minorities. It is in Turkey's interest to improve these conditions, considering the economic benefits of integration. The membership of Turkey in the EU would be advantageous to both parties economically and vital to European security. Turkey's military strength and geostrategic position between Europe and the Middle East make the country an ideal ally in the 21st century.

Germany favors Turkey's accession to the EU, whereas some in France object. This might be due to Germany's large number of Muslim immigrants, as opposed to the fear of "cultural intrusion" in France. Overall, the arguments favoring integration prevail. Although Turkey's democratic system has shortcomings, membership in the EU would refute images of a "clash of civilizations" and lessen the security threat from fundamentalist Muslim states.

Although Turkey's mainland is located in Asia and only a fragment of its largest city is situated on the European continent, the Republic of Turkey was founded solely on European principles in 1923. Furthermore, Kemal Ataturk, the founder of Turkey, could not have imagined a civilized Turkey without its European affiliation: "The West has always been prejudiced against the Turks . . . but we Turks have always consistently moved towards the West. In order to be a civilized nation, there is no alternative" (Erdogdu 40). These words display the long-felt desire of the Turkish people to be an integrated part of Europe and the historical connection between Europe and Turkey. Relations between the Turks and the Europeans date back to the 11th century, when the Ottoman Empire extended all the way to Vienna. With the expansion of trade routes in the 16th century, Turks and Europeans established vital trade relations, which eventually led to extensive diplomatic exchanges in the beginning of the 19th century.

Since then Turkish governments have been encouraging a process of "Westernization" to prepare for even stronger political and economic ties with Europe (Erdogdu 41). Indeed, Turkey is a member state of all European intergovernmental organizations except the European Union (EU). Turkey signed an agreement with the European Economic Community in 1963. Moreover, the country was a founding member of the United Nations, a longtime member of the NATO, and a partner in the Customs Union. Nevertheless,

Turkey has repeatedly been denied membership in the EU, which has cited its unstable democracy and its record of human rights violations as the reasons. Despite these legitimate reservations about Turkey's adherence to European principles, such as democracy and human rights, the EU should admit Turkey in order to build a secure and culturally diverse Europe.

According to Birol Yesilada, Turkey's involvement with the EU began in the late 1950's, when Turkey applied for an associate membership in the European Economic Community. This membership was granted in the Ankara Agreement of 1963, but relations worsened after military interventions in 1971 and 1980 overthrew the civil government (94–95). The first time Turkey applied for membership in the EU was in 1987. Turgut Ozal, then Turkish Prime Minister, stated that the membership application would "eliminate any ambiguity by anchoring once and for all the destiny of the Turkish people with that of the Western people" (Featherstone and Kazemis 283). Although Turkey's application was rejected because of political instability, the EU and Turkey signed a Customs Union agreement in 1995 that allowed extended economic cooperation and to Turks, symbolized Turkey's membership in Europe (Yesilada 95).

In 1997, the relations between Turkey and Europe had deteriorated, and the Luxembourg summit decided that Turkey would be excluded from the candidate list for EU membership. The Commission demanded political and economic reforms, improvement in human rights, and improvement of relations with Greece. Turkey's pride was damaged by this decision, and relations with the EU cooled down for two years (Yesilada 95). In light of the devastating 1999 earthquakes in Turkey, Europe and Turkey made another effort to resolve their differences. That same year, the Commission recommended the inclusion of Turkey as a candidate for integration without giving a specific date for accession talks to begin. At the European Council meeting in Nice in 2000, both sides agreed to develop a roadmap for implementing necessary reforms. Turkey, in turn, presented a National Program or reform plan, and a year later the government proposed 37 amendments to the Constitution to show its "commitment to meet the democratization requirements of EU membership" (Yesilada 99).

In fact, the EU has formally outlined membership requirements, known as the Copenhagen Criteria, which include "Europeanness, political criteria, and economic criteria" (Yesilada 100). However, this long history of Turkey's futile attempts towards membership in the EU demonstrates that "European Identity" is not measured only by economic and political success, but also in terms of geographical, cultural, historical, and religious criteria. As Huntington writes in regard to the continued rejection of Turkey by the EU, ". . . the real reasons were the intense opposition of the

Greeks and, more importantly, the fact that Turkey is a Muslim country (Huntington 146).

The current debate on the process of accession for Turkey brings forward the arguments of both supporters and opponents of Turkey's membership in the EU. Opponents of Turkey's integration, like Valery Giscard d'Estaing, former French president, have three arguments against the accession process. The first argument is that Turkey is not only geographically detached, but also culturally and religiously dissimilar. These views might stem from the historical European fear of Islamic conquest. Giscard d'Estaing, whose task was to write the new EU constitution, warned politicians that the membership of Turkey would mean "the end of the European Union." He stated that Turkey's capital "is not in Europe, 95 per cent of its population is outside Europe, it is not a European country" (Boulton and Parker). He believes that other EU members secretly have the same reservations. Among his supporters is former socialist French foreign minister Hubert Vedrine (Boulton and Parker). The second concern expressed by opponents is the potential flood of immigrants from Turkey, given its population of 70 million inhabitants. The third argument is that Turkey's economy is struggling and will only be a burden on the European Union's budget (Wysling).

Advocates argue that Turkey's membership in the EU is of "strategic importance" since it is a leading regional power in the Middle East and serves as a major route for future oil transport (Wysling). Supporters of the future membership of Turkey in the EU include Britain, Germany, Greece, and Denmark (Boulton and Parker). Germany is the biggest single trade partner of Turkey, accounting for an "average of 20 to 25 per cent of annual exports and 15 to 18 per cent of annual imports" (Yesilada 107). Given these circumstances and in view of its large Muslim population, Germany's stance on this issue is not solely driven by concern for international security and peace but by economics. Advocates also point out the potential danger of not accepting Turkey's candidacy. As Erdogdu states: "If Turkey is left alone it might be prey to radical Islamic forces" (44). In fact, Gen. Tuncer Kilinc, the General Secretary of the National Security Council in Turkey, indicated that Turkey should look for new allies. He said: "It would be useful if Turkey engaged in a search that would involve Russia and Iran" (Unal).

The Commission in charge of the EU's enlargement process should seize this unique chance of cooperating with a Muslim country in order to defeat anti-Western sentiment and terrorism and to spread democratization in the East. Turkey's population is 99 percent Islamic, but the state has been fundamentally secular for seventy years. Islam in Turkey is far from being an "effective regulator of political and economic life" (Balkir and Williams 225). Although there had been a rise of radical Islamic movements in the 1970's and 1980's, Turkey's anti-Saddam position in the Gulf War and its close alliance with the West have had an impact on the Islamic movement within the country. "It's been speculated that the decline in the number of and circulation of Islamist periodicals and journals since the Gulf War has been due to the decrease in the financial support supplied by the Saudi and Gulf State sources to the Islamists in Turkey" (Balkir and Williams 229). However, rejection by the EU could result in increased domination by the Islamists.

Europeans often find it a contradiction in terms that Turkey, a Muslim country, is a secular democracy with a market economy (Müftüler-Bac 12). But Turkey defines itself as a modern, multicultural, multireligious, and multiethnic society. "Such concepts as liberty, property, individual rights and liberalism" were introduced to society as early as the 18th century, following the enforcement of Western European legal, administrative and political systems (Müftüler-Bac 16). It should be evident to the European Commission that Turkey stands out among other Muslim nations as secular and democratic. In addition, Turkey has a long record as a NATO ally, and its integration into the EU would send an important signal to the world, namely that Europeans are open to both Muslim and Christian societies. "It would symbolize a much-needed embrace of the Islamic world" (Teitelbaum 97). It would also have great meaning to the "11 to 12 million Muslims in Europe, including 5 million in France, 3 million in Germany, 2 million in the UK, and 1 million in Italy" (Teitelbaum 97).

Before Turkey can be granted membership in the EU, it has to adhere to European human rights regulations and improve its treatment of minorities. Regarding human rights violations, the EU is concerned with Turkey's use of torture and ill treatment of prisoners, rule of law, freedom of expression, and respect for Kurdish citizens. "Precise cases of torture and ill-treatment have been recently registered by a delegation of the European Committee for the Prevention of Torture and Inhuman or Degrading Treatment or Punishment," stated the European Commission after its visit in 1999 (Yesilada 105). The EU also requires the abolition of the death penalty prior to Turkey's membership. Turkey has restricted the death penalty to crimes of terrorism but has not banned it completely (Yesilada 105). Furthermore, freedom of speech is still very limited in Turkey. Political parties that openly deal with the Kurdish issue or advocate radical left-wing views face censure for being unconstitutional and are usually banned. In 1998, the European Court unanimously found a violation by Turkey of the Convention regarding the dissolution of a political party (Poulton 47–62). Additional undemocratic tendencies can be seen in the exaggerated power that the military, namely the National Security Council, has over civilian institutions. The civilian government has been overthrown by guards of the National Security Council three times since 1960 (Featherstone and Kazemis 257).

In its latest meeting, the EU Parliament urged Turkey to fully implement the reforms suggested by the Commission and to make additional efforts towards development of "a democracy consistent with European standards" (Europa: Relations with Turkey). Turkey took offense at the assumption that, according to the EU Commission, it was considered less democratic than the post-Cold-War regimes of Eastern Europe (Featherstone and Kazemis 258). However, after its exclusion from the list of future EU candidate states in 1997, Turkey had been decreasing its commitment to democratization and freedom of expression. In 1999, the Ministry of Interior banned "the use of certain terminology in relation to the Kurdish question in press releases and publications" (Yesilada 106). The same year, the Court of Appeals lengthened the sentences for abuse of freedom of speech. Up until 2001, TV broadcasting in Kurdish was not allowed and foreign language schools (e.g., Kurdish) were forbidden (Yesilada 107). But thanks to its new status as a candidate for integration, Turkey's government is making an effort to change its human rights situation in order to meet the Copenhagen criteria. For example, the Turkish parliament is considering a Penal Code bill that abolishes the death penalty, in accordance with EU policy (Yesilada 104).

Although the EU should insist on the fulfillment of its political pre-requisites for accession, it should not lose sight of the role Turkey could play in enhancing Europe's security network. Turkey has a strategic position between Europe and the Middle East and would be considered a vital regional ally at a time when Arab public opinion has turned anti-Western and fears of regional instability have increased. As a reliable, democratic participant in international affairs, Turkey should be an essential part of the European security structure (Aybet 103–10). According to Samuel Huntington's theory of a "clash of civilizations," future conflicts will evolve more and more around religious and ethnic differences (Huntington 28–29, 217–18). In this case, Turkey's "geopolitical position" could shift towards the Middle East, making it a vital ally for the West. In times of increasingly anti-American sentiment among Arabs, its military agreement with Israel in 1996 demonstrated its loyalty to the West. Furthermore, Turkey could provide an alternative to Russian models of democracy for former Soviet States.

Another important security aspect to be considered in the accession process is Turkey's potential role in the European Security and Defense Policy (ESDP). Turkey could contribute greatly to improved defense technology and increased troops for the ESDP since it spends 14% of its budget on defense (McBride) and invested $31 billion dollars for the modernization of its army (Gorvett 32). Turkey's 600,000-strong army is the second largest standing army in NATO, and its soldiers are very experienced in fighting (Gorvett 32). Turkey's membership would thus be advantageous in that it could help Europe to build up a credible military force comparable to NATO. In short, an integration of Turkey would result in positive changes for European security.

Turkey is in the process of creating a stable market economy, and its accession into the EU would benefit both parties' economic development. Almost all other potential members have weaker economies than Turkey, which has the sixteenth largest economy in the world, profiting from a growing consumer market and "a dynamic private sector that competes successfully in world markets" (Yesilada 107). The EU is Turkey's primary trade and investment partner, making up 50% of Turkey's foreign trade (Yesilada 107). Turkey's economy also serves as a bridge between European and Central Asian markets, so Turkey is attractive to foreign investors (Yesilada 108). For Turkey, the prospect of a flourishing economy as a full member of the European Union could result in increased efforts to move towards a fully democratic society that respects human rights and tolerates minorities. Turkey is clearly willing to implement major legal reforms in exchange for an extended economic partnership. In that respect, Europeans have the leverage to make a change in Turkey's interior politics if they are willing to allow the integration of Turkey into the EU.

It can be argued that Turkey's process of democratization has not sufficiently fulfilled the requirements for EU membership. However, the reform packages that the Turkish government introduced in August 2002 include the following changes in law:

The expression of opinion will no longer face criminal sanctions, broadcasting and education in other languages is now authorized, gender equality has been improved and the competence of the State Security Courts narrowed. Furthermore, training courses in human rights have been offered for judges and law enforcement officials. (Commission of the Europe Communities, 2002 Regular Report)

This list of alterations to Turkey's civilian institutions and laws proves the government's willingness to move towards an adoption of European standards in order to realize its long desired membership in the EU. An improvement in Turkey's democratization is, of course, not the only benefit resulting from an integration of Turkey into the EU. From an economic perspective, Turkey's accession would extend European markets and increase foreign trade. Furthermore, Turkey is vital to the security interests of the EU, given the fact that despite its Muslim background, it has acted as a reliable Western ally. Therefore, Turkey should be integrated into the EU even though the weakness of Turkey's democracy has been under scrutiny. Its membership would refute images of a "clash of civilizations" and would lessen the security threat from fundamentalist Muslim states. The EU needs Turkey to achieve security and cultural diversity in Europe.

(2,540 words)

Works Cited

Aybet, Gulnur. "Turkey and European Institutions." *The International Spectator* 34.1 (Jan.-Mar. 1999): 103–10.

Balkir, Canan, and Allan M. Williams, eds. *Turkey and Europe.* London: Pinter, 1993.

Boulton, Leyla, and George Parker. "Ankara Bid to Join EU Attacked by Giscard." *Financial Times* 9 Nov. 2002.

Erdogdu, Erkan. "Turkey and Europe: Undivided but Not United." *Middle Eastern Review of International Affairs* 6.2 (2002): 40–49.

Featherstone, Kevin, and George Kazemis, eds. *Europeanization and the Southern Periphery.* London: Frank Cass, 2001.

Gorvett, Jon. "As EU Membership Beckons, Turkey's Military Faces Difficult Choice." *The Washington Report on Middle East Affairs* 22.6 (July-Aug. 2003): 30.

———. "IMF-Backed Reforms Separate Economy from Politics, Face Opposition of Turkey's Ruling Elites." *The Washington Report on Middle East Affairs* 20.5 (31 July 2001): 31–33.

Huntington, Samuel P. *The Clash of Civilizations and the Remaking of the World Order.* New York: Simon & Schuster, 1996.

McBride, Edward. "Survey: Turkey—Last Line of Defence." *The Economist* 355 (10 June 2000): T13–14.

Müftüler-Bac, Meltem. *Turkey's Relations with a Changing Europe.* New York: St. Martin's Press, 1997.

Poulton, Hugh. "The Turkish State and Democracy." *The International Spectator* 34.1 (Jan.-Mar. 1999): 47–62.

"Relations with Turkey." Europa: European Commission: Enlargement Homepage. 21 Mar. 2003. <http://www.europa.eu.int/comm/enlargement/turkey/index.htm>.

Teitelbaum, Michael S., and Philip L. Martin. "Is Turkey Ready for Europe?" *Foreign Affairs* 82.3 (May-June 2003): 97.

Unal, Elef. "Polarization Deepens in Turkey over EU." *Turkish Daily News* (10 Mar. 2002).

Wood, David M., and Birol A. Yesilada. *The Emerging European Union.* New York: Longman, 2002.

Wysling, Andreas. "Turkey and Europe: A Tale of Two Complexes." *Neue Zuericher Zeitung* (10 Apr. 2003).

Yesilada, Birol A. "Turkey's Candidacy for EU Membership." *The Middle East Journal* 56.1 (Winter 2002): 94–111.

Note: Some online sources do not have page numbers, so the in-text citations include only the last name(s) of the author(s).

Sentence Outline: "Turkey's Integration into the European Union (EU)"

I. Introduction
    A. Background: _____
    B. Thesis: _____

II. Major Point
    A. _____
    B. _____

III. Major Point
    A. _____
    B. _____

IV. Major Point
    A. _____
    B. _____

V. Major Point
    A. _____
    B. _____

VI. Major Point
    A. _____
    B. _____

VII. Major Point
    A. _____
    B. _____

VIII. Major Point
    A. _____
    B. _____

IX. Conclusion
    A. Summary: _____
    B. Summary: _____
    C. Thesis Re-statement _____

ASSIGNMENT   Research Paper

Write a research paper on the topic you chose on page 166 or another topic that you want to investigate. Complete the Preliminary Research form on page 167, and the Research Proposal on page 172 before beginning to write. While you are writing and editing your paper, aim for clarity, coherence, conciseness, and precision in your document. Include graphic aids (charts, tables, graphs, photographs, and maps) to enhance the impact of the document. These graphic aids may be inserted in the body or the appendix, depending on their size and purpose. Be sure to title the graphic aids and cite their sources.

In your paper, use the Modern Language Association (MLA) style for citation, which is preferred for papers written in the humanities, including English and foreign languages. In this style, the author's last name and the page number where the information is located are given within parentheses following the quotation or paraphrase: (Lowell 258). List all your sources at the end of your paper under Works Cited, alphabetizing them by the author's last name. If no author is identified, alphabetize the sources by the first word of the title, not including *a*, *an*, or *the*.

Duke University provides a Guide to Library Research with comprehensive information about citation rules under Citing Sources (Citing Sources and Avoiding Plagiarism: Documentation Guidelines) at *www.lib.duke.edu/libguide/*. For the rules on citation of electronic sources, see Citation Styles: Using MLA Style to Cite and Document Sources in Online! at *www.bedfordstmartins.com/online/cite5.html/*.

Components of a Research Paper

When submitting the final draft, place it in a folder or a binder with the components in this order:

- Title Page
- Abstract
- Table of Contents
- Body of Paper
- Appendix
- Works Cited

Evaluator _____

Author _____

RESEARCH PAPER EVALUATION FORM

Excellent +   **Satisfactory √**   **Unsatisfactory –**

Content
- Proof of argument
- Logic of development   _____
- Synthesis of information   _____
                                                           _____

Organization
- Thesis in introduction
- Topic sentences   _____
- Paragraph and paper coherence   _____
                                                           _____

Style
- Paraphrasing
- Use of quotations   _____
- Clarity, conciseness, precision   _____
                                                           _____

Mechanics
- Standard English grammar
- Punctuation, capitalization, spelling   _____
- Citation of sources   _____
                                                           _____

Format
- Paragraphing
- Spacing and margins   _____
- Page numbers   _____
                                                           _____

Documentation
- Form of citations
- Number of citations   _____
- Works Cited   _____
                                                           _____

Overall Evaluation: _____

Comments _____

_____

CHAPTER

13

Your Authentic Voice

This final chapter discusses discovering your authentic voice, capitalizing on your unique creative abilities, and enjoying the experience of writing. Of course, the term *writer's voice* is somewhat abstract, but simply put, it refers to the particular style, tone, texture, and quality of an individual's writing. While your style can change superficially, depending on the purpose of your writing, your essential voice remains the same. According to Louis Menand, writing in *The New Yorker* (June 28, 2004):

> One of the most mysterious of writing's immaterial properties is what people call "voice." Editors sometimes refer to it, in a phrase that underscores the paradox at the heart of the idea, as "the voice on the page". . . . Writing that has a voice is writing that has something like a personality.[1]

In connection with appreciating your writer's voice, this chapter also explains the importance of avoiding plagiarism, which is a serious crime in the United States and other countries. Plagiarism is the act of using another person's words or ideas without giving credit to the original author. The principles that underlie the rules on plagiarism are these:

- Each individual is the owner of his or her own ideas/words.
- Respect must be accorded to the person who originates ideas/words.
- Citation of sources is the legal method to attribute words/ideas taken from others.
  - ➤ Place quotation marks around words, phrases, and sentences copied exactly from a text, and provide documentation (footnotes or in-text citations).
  - ➤ Provide documentation (footnotes or in-text citations) for words, phrases, and sentences that are paraphrased.
  - ➤ Provide a list of Works Cited (also called References or Bibliography) at the end of the document.

Duke University offers a Guide to Library Research with comprehensive information about citation rules under Citing Sources (Citing Sources and Avoiding Plagiarism: Documentation Guidelines) at *www.lib.duke.edu/libguide/*. For the rules on citation of electronic sources, see Citation Styles: Using MLA Style to Cite and Document Sources in Online! at *www.bedfordstmartins.com/online/cite5.html/*.

---

[1] Louis Menand, "Bad Comma," *The New Yorker*, June 28, 2004, 103–4.

STRATEGIES

Experience

No two people have the same writing style, just as no two people, even twins, have the same fingerprint. It is, therefore, not likely that one person would write exactly like another. But certainly it is difficult to find an authentic voice, and becoming a skillful writer is a gradual process of trial and error. The more experience in writing you have, the better writer you will be. As you have completed the various writing tasks in this textbook, you have made progress and broadened your experience.

Writing is a skill, and like any other skill, it tends to improve with steady practice. The best writers have discovered and refined their unique voices through dedication to writing. Without taking such an extreme approach, you can enhance and make use of your inborn writing talent by writing as often and as much as possible, for instance, keeping a daily journal, as mentioned in Chapter 3, Writer's Block. The more you write, the more you will begin to enjoy the intellectual and emotional rewards of transforming thoughts into words. Still, no one can deny that writing is hard work. Becoming a good writer takes time and effort, along with steady concentration, strong motivation, and a little luck. Even then, you may need patience. As the author Louis Menand says: "Composition is a troublesome, balky, sometimes sleep-depriving business. What makes it especially so is that the rate of production is beyond the writer's control. You have to wait, and what you are waiting for is something inside you to come up with the words. That something, for writers, is the voice."[2]

Confidence

This textbook offers writing guidelines, accepted principles, and practical strategies to those who want to improve their writing. While using this book, you have probably experimented with these strategies to find the ones that are most helpful to you. But whether or not you continue to follow the suggestions in this book, you now know a great deal about writing. As an author, you understand the benefits of sharpening your focus on your goal, outlining your ideas, and editing and rewriting your first draft. You are pre-

[2] Ibid., 104.

pared to make well-informed choices about the format, organization, content, and style of your documents.

While becoming comfortable with the writing process, you have seen your voice evolve, and when you sit at your desk and begin to write, it is your style and personality that fill the page. Because your writing style is part of who you are, even as it develops and changes over the years, it will continue to embody your personal characteristics. It is these special characteristics that energize writing and make the writer's voice memorable. The individuality and originality of a writer are primary aspects of good writing

Excellence in writing is, finally, a mysterious quality that defies explanation. It results from an unequal mixture of inborn talent, acquired skills, and personal effort. If you believe in your natural talent, acquire the necessary skills, and make a strong effort, you can achieve excellence.

Evaluation: What Is Plagiarism?

Read the paragraph from a 2004 editorial in *BusinessWeek* titled "The Working Poor: We Can Do Better." Then read the two rewrites of the original paragraph. With your classmates, discuss whether these rewrites should be considered plagiarism, and explain your reasoning. Does the fact that the rewrites include a footnote affect your opinion?

Original:
The Working Poor: We Can Do Better

"What can be done to reduce the ranks of the working poor? The best remedy would be another boom like the one the U.S. had in the 1990s. But wages at the bottom aren't likely to rise until the unemployment rate, now at 5.6%, drops below 5% and stays there for a sustained period—something that's not likely to happen for a while."[3]

[3] "The Working Poor: We Can Do Better," *BusinessWeek*, May 31, 2004, 108.

Rewrite 1:
The Working Poor: We Can Do Better

What can we do to reduce the number of poor workers? The best solution is another growth period like the one in the U.S. during the 1990s. But wages at the bottom probably won't rise until the unemployment rate, currently at 5.6%, falls below 5% and stays there for a long time—which may not happen for a while.[4]

Rewrite 2:
The Working Poor: We Can Do Better

Can anything be done so that the ranks of the working poor will be reduced? If the U.S. had another boom like the one in the 1990s, that would be the best remedy. But it's not likely that wages at the bottom will rise until the unemployment rate, now at 5.6%, drops below 5% and remains at that rate for a sustained period—something that's not going to happen for a while.[5]

[4] Ibid.
[5] Ibid.

ASSIGNMENT   Summary—"The Working Poor: We Can Do Better"

After reading the editorial from *BusinessWeek* (May 31, 2004) "The Working Poor: We Can Do Better," write a 150-word summary of it. In your summary, paraphrase the content, and also include a few quotations. After you have completed your first draft, exchange summaries with a classmate and evaluate them, using the plagiarism prevention form.

Evaluator _____

Author _____

Plagiarism Prevention

Excellent +   **Satisfactory √**   **Unsatisfactory –**

- The writer has paraphrased the statements (words, phrases, sentences) in the original document.   _____

- Synonyms are substituted for the original words in the paraphrases.   _____

- The original sentence structure is changed in the paraphrases.   _____

- The paraphrases preserve the meaning of the original statements.   _____

- A few key quotations are included within quotation marks.   _____

- Paraphrases and quotations are followed by an in-text citation of source.   _____

- Technical words and terms are not paraphrased.   _____

- The source in the document is listed by title in Works Cited.   _____

Editorial

The Working Poor: We Can Do Better[6]

The boom and bust of the past 10 years left many Americans better off. Incomes and wealth are way up, and the unemployment rate is almost a percentage point lower than it was in 1994. But despite these gains, far too many American workers are still stuck in low-paying jobs, with few or no benefits (page 58). More than 28 million people—about a quarter of the workforce age 18 to 64—earned less than $9.04 an hour in 2003. That translates into a full-time income of $18,800 a year or less, which is the weighted poverty line for a family of four.

What can be done to reduce the ranks of the working poor? The best remedy would be another boom like the one the U.S. had in the 1990s. But wages at the bottom aren't likely to rise until the unemployment rate, now at 5.6%, drops below 5% and stays there for a sustainable period— something that's not likely to happen for a while.

Raising the minimum wage is an option that would help many low-wage workers. It was hiked twice in the 1990s, from $4.25 an hour at the beginning of 1996 to $5.15 an hour by the end of 1997. Since then, inflation has pushed down the value of the minimum wage to its early 1996 level in real terms. So it needs to be boosted again, at least enough to keep up with inflation. Such an increase would clearly help the bottom rung of the workforce. True, many economists worry that a higher minimum wage would discourage hiring of less educated Americans. But the minimum-wage hikes of the 1990s appear to have had little impact on job prospects for low-end workers.

The government should also substantially increase aid for higher education. In an era when post–high school education is almost essential to compete in the global economy, talented young people shouldn't be kept from college for financial reasons. In recent years tuition has gone up sharply, especially at financially stressed public universities, while Federal Pell Grants to low-income college students have not kept up. The working poor would also benefit from

[6] Ibid.

reforms of the U.S. health-care system, which in its current state makes it difficult for marginal workers to get medical coverage. A wholesale overhaul won't happen soon, but it may be feasible to help poor workers obtain catastrophic coverage.

Technology, globalization, and immigration provide enormous benefits for the economy, but the costs are often borne by the lowest-paid members of the workforce. If there are simple, straightforward ways to improve the lot of America's working poor without impeding growth, we as a nation have an obligation to try.

ANALYSIS: THE WRITER'S VOICE— *AN AMERICAN CHILDHOOD*

The passage on page 205 is taken from *An American Childhood* by Annie Dillard, a contemporary author who often writes about nature and the environment. In this memoir, Dillard examines her life as a child growing up in Pittsburgh, Pennsylvania. In the excerpt, the author explains how she gradually became familiar with the world outside her neighborhood. Read this excerpt aloud with your classmates; then discuss the techniques that characterize this writer's unique and vivid voice. Consider these questions in your analysis, and underline examples in the text that support your answers:

- What are the characteristics of this writer's style?
- What is the tone of this excerpt?
- What pronouns does the author use?
- What adjectives and adverbs does the author use?
- Does the author use strong, active verbs?
- Does the author use a variety of sentence structures?
- Where does the author use parallelism?
- Explain the author's use of metaphors.

An American Childhood: Part One[7]

Walking was my project before reading. The text I read was the town; the book I made up was a map. First I had walked across one of our side yards to the blackened alley with its buried dime. Now I walked to piano lessons, four long blocks north of school and three zigzag blocks into an Irish neighborhood near Thomas Boulevard.

I pushed at my map's edges. Alone at night I added newly memorized streets and blocks to old streets and blocks, and imagined connecting them on foot. From my parents' earliest injunctions I felt that my life depended on keeping it all straight—remembering where on earth I lived, that is, in relation to where I had walked. It was dead reckoning. On dark evenings I came home exultant, secretive, often from some exotic leafy curb a mile beyond what I had known at lunch, where I had peered up at the street sign, hugging the cold pole, and fixed the intersection in my mind. What joy, what relief, eased me as I pushed open the heavy front door!—joy and relief because, from the very trackless waste, I had located home, family, and the dinner table once again.

[7] Annie Dillard, *An American Childhood* (New York: HarperCollins, 1987), 44.

ANALYSIS: THE WRITER'S VOICE—
LOOKING FOR SPINOZA

The passage that follows is taken from *Looking for Spinoza: Joy, Sorrow, and the Feeling Brain* by Antonio Damasio. In this book, Damasio, a neuroscientist, examines the nature of feelings and explains how they support human survival. After reading this excerpt, analyze the unique voice of this author, who has the ability to explain complex scientific concepts in simple language.

Consider these questions in your evaluation, and underline examples in the text that support your answers:

- What are the characteristics of this writer's style?
- Which statements reveal the personal feelings of the author?
- What is the tone of this excerpt?
- What pronouns does the author use?
- What adjectives and adverbs does the author use?
- Does the author use strong, active verbs?
- Does the author use a variety of sentence structures?
- Where does the author use parallelism?
- Explain the author's use of metaphors.

Looking for Spinoza: Joy, Sorrow, and the Feeling Brain[8]

Chapter 1: Enter Feelings

Feelings of pain or pleasure or some quality in between are the bedrock of our minds. We often fail to notice this simple reality because the mental images of the objects and events that surround us, along with the images of the words and sentences that describe them, use up so much of our overburdened attention. But there they are, feelings of myriad emotions and related states, the continuous musical line

---

[8] Antonio Damasio, *Looking for Spinoza: Joy, Sorrow, and the Feeling Brain* (New York: Harcourt, Inc., 2003), 3–4.

of our minds, the unstoppable humming of the most universal of melodies that only dies down when we go to sleep, a humming that turns into all-out singing when we are occupied by joy, or a mournful requiem when sorrow takes over.

Given the ubiquity of feelings, one would have thought that their science would have been elucidated long ago—what feelings are, how they work, what they mean—but that is hardly the case. Of all the mental phenomena we can describe, feelings and their essential ingredients—pain and pleasure—are the least understood in biological and specifically neurobiological terms. This is all the more puzzling considering that advanced societies cultivate feelings shamelessly and dedicate so many resources and efforts to manipulating those feelings with alcohol, drugs of abuse, medical drugs, food, real sex, virtual sex, all manner of feel-good consumption, and all manner of feel-good social and religious practices. We doctor our feelings with pills, drinks, health spas, workouts, and spiritual exercises, but neither the public nor science have yet come to grips with what feelings are, biologically speaking.

I am not really surprised at this state of affairs, considering what I grew up believing about feelings. Most of it simply was not true. For example, I thought that feelings were impossible to define with specificity, unlike objects you could see, hear, or touch. Unlike those concrete entities, feelings were intangible. When I started musing about how the brain managed to create the mind, I accepted the established advice that feelings were out of the scientific picture. One could study how the brain makes us move. One could study sensory processes, visual and otherwise, and understand how thoughts are put together. One could study how the brain learns and memorizes thoughts. One could even study the emotional reactions with which we respond to varied objects and events. But feelings—which can be distinguished from emotions . . . —remained elusive. Feelings were to stay forever mysterious. They were private and inaccessible. It was not possible to explain how feelings happened or where they happened. One simply could not get "behind" feelings.

ANALYSIS: THE WRITER'S VOICE— "A DREAM VACATION IN SWITZERLAND"

Read the personal research essay "A Dream Vacation in Switzerland" on pages 209–211, and evaluate the uniqueness of the writer's voice. Consider thse questions in your evaluation, and underline examples in the text that support your answers:

- What are the characteristics of this writer's style?
- Which statements reveal the personal feelings of the author?
- What is the tone of this essay?
- What sentence connectors does the author use?
- What pronouns does the author use?
- What adjectives and adverbs does the author use?
- Does the author use strong, active verbs?
- Does the author use a variety of sentence structures?
- Where does the author use parallelism?
- Has the author effectively incorporated information from sources into the essay?

Essay

A Dream Vacation in Switzerland

HOON JEONG

When I was young boy growing up in Korea, I dreamed of traveling all around the world. My father was the captain of a huge trading vessel, so he visited many countries. Whenever he came back from trading in a country, he brought me fascinating souvenirs like postcards and stamps, which showed me many beautiful places in the world where I had never been. I saw wonderful scenery on these postcards, and I realized that the pictures were taken in European countries, and quite often in Switzerland, in central Europe. Also, several of my closest friends, who liked to vacation in Europe, said that Switzerland was an especially fascinating country because it was completely different from Korea in almost every way. Now I would like to take a vacation in Switzerland to climb the vast Swiss Alps, enjoy the lovely lakes, and visit the great museums and archeological sites.

Switzerland is a unique country, culturally, economically, and politically. It is small in size, like Korea, but has a population of only 7.5 million. The people are wealthy and well educated: the GDP was $32,000 in 2002, and the literacy rate is now 99 percent (CIA World Factbook). More than four languages are spoken there, including German, French, Italian, and Romansch. This is because various ethnic groups live in Switzerland, unlike Korea, which has a homogeneous population. Germans make up 65 percent of the total, and French are the next largest group at 18 percent. Then come the Italians at 10 percent and the Romansch at 1 percent (CIA World Factbook). The currency is the Swiss franc since Switzerland is one of the few European countries that does not use the Euro. Another interesting fact about this country is that it is committed to neutrality and did not take part in World Wars I and II. Nevertheless, it has been deeply involved with the United Nations although it did not formally join until 2002 (CIA World Factbook).

I plan on seeing a variety of famous sites in Switzerland, starting from Interlaken, where the Alps are located. Even though I'm hardly an expert in mountain climbing, I love the fresh air and the incredible view from the top of a high mountain, so I want to climb the Alps. Then, I will visit Lakes Lucerne, Geneva, and Maggiore. Besides this gorgeous scenery, Switzerland has a large number of world-class museums, for example, the Beyeler Foundation of the Arts in Basel and the Museum of the History of Transport, (road, rail, aviation, astronautics) in Lucerne. I also want to visit the Picasso Museum in Lucerne, which has a fine collection of Picassos as well as hundreds of photographs of the artist. Finally, I will tour the Augusta Raurica, an archeological ruin, which was built by the Romans in 44 BC and has a well-preserved Roman-style theater (Switzerlandisyours.com).

Of course, I would love to travel around the world, as my father did on his ship, and, whenever possible, I hope to spend time at the ocean, watching the powerful natural beauty of the tides. However, Switzerland is one of the most attractive countries in the world, and I am putting this country first in my choice of places to visit on a dream vacation. The Swiss people welcome tourists, the scenery varies from lakes to mountains, and the cultural attractions and archeological sites appeal to me. For all these reasons, I expect that someday soon my journey to Switzerland will be not only a dream but also a reality.

Works Cited

"Museums." Switzerland.isyours.com. 2005. Michelaud & Co. <www.Switzerlandisyours.com.>
"Switzerland." Central Intelligence Agency, The World Factbook. 2005. 10 Feb. 2005. <www.cia.gov>.

 ASSIGNMENT **Personal Research Essay**

Write an essay of about 600 words in which you describe a place that you would like to visit if you could take a vacation anywhere in the world. Do research on the Internet to find information on this location, and incorporate this information into your essay. Include a photograph or a map of the location with your paper.

In your paper, use the Modern Language Association (MLA) style for citation, which is preferred for papers written in the humanities, including English and foreign languages. In this style, the author's last name and the page number where the information is located are given within parentheses following the quotation or paraphrase: (Lowell 258). List all your sources at the end of your paper under Works Cited, alphabetizing them by the author's last name. If no author is identified, alphabetize the sources by the first word of the title, not including *a*, *an*, or *the*.

The Pleasure of Writing

Prepare an outline before writing.

Listen to your writer's voice.

Ensure that grammar and mechanics are correct.

Avoid redundancy.

Select the precise word to convey your meaning.

Use sentence combining, sentence connectors, and active verbs.

Rewrite your first draft.

Enjoy the writing process.

Definitions of Writing Terms

Abstract: A short summary of the main ideas and topics of a research paper, report, journal article, or technical document, which appears before the document and is usually 250 words or less.

Analogy: Similarity in some respects between things otherwise unlike.

> **Example:**
> "Like an old married couple, the Americans and Europeans bicker about relatively minor issues, but make sure that their broader trade relationship does not break down" ("Trade Disputes: Dangerous Activities," *The Economist,* May 11, 2002, 64).

Analysis: Breaking up a whole into its parts and examining these parts to solve a problem or reach a conclusion.

Argument: An essay in which the writer presents a point of view and attempts to persuade others of the validity of his or her opinion.

Business Letter: Common form of external business correspondence, usually sent from a representative of an organization to people outside the organization.

Case Study: Method of instruction that is used in American business school and involves the analysis of actual business situations to teach problem solving.

Critical Review: An essay based on critical reading of a text, in which the writer summarizes, reacts to, and evaluates an author's ideas. Also called a critique or reaction paper.

Deductive Organization: Placement of the main idea of a text at the beginning. The writer gives the conclusion first and then presents supporting evidence.

Deductive Restatement Organization: Placement of the main idea of a text at the beginning and again at the end. The repeated main idea is often a paraphrased version of the original.

Essay: An analytical or interpretive composition that deals with its subject in a limited way.

Figure of Speech: An expression (metaphor or simile) using words in a nonliteral or unusual sense to add vividness to what is said and comparing dissimilar objects or ideas.

Format: The general arrangement or plan of a document; the physical presentation of a document on the page.

Gender-Neutral Language: Language that shows no gender bias. It does not use the false generics *man* and *mankind* to represent both males and females (substituting *humankind, humans,* or *human beings*) and prefers *he or she* and *his or her* to *he* and *his*. Also called non-sexist language.

Examples:

The average American has seen a decline in his or her economic status.

Laura has dedicated her life to helping humankind.

Idiom: An accepted phrase or expression that is contrary to the usual patterns of the language or that has a meaning different from the literal meaning of the words.

Example:

"Realizing your dream will always take longer and suck up more resources than you planned, and the process can drive well-meaning people around the bend" (Frank Batten, "Out of the Blue and into the Black," *Harvard Business Review* 80, no. 4 [April 2002]: 113).

Inductive Organization: Placement of the main idea of a text at the end; the writer gives supporting evidence and leads the reader to a conclusion.

In-Text Citation System: Citation system for documenting sources in a research paper, report, essay, journal article, or technical document; the author's last name and the page number are placed within parentheses in the text (Martin 123). All sources are listed as Works Cited at the end of the document.

Irony: A method of humorous or sarcastic expression in which the intended meaning of the words used is the direct opposite of their usual sense.

Example:

"The board of directors is supposed to carefully calibrate compensation packages so that CEOs are paid just enough to be motivated to swing their weary legs out of bed each morning and clomp to work" (Randall E. Stross, "Masters of the Universe," *U.S. News & World Report,* May 27, 2002, 41).

Main Idea: The most important idea or unifying theme of a paragraph or longer text.

Memorandum: An informal written business communication, usually from one person or department to another within an organization.

Metaphor: A figure of speech in which a thing, idea, or action is referred to by a word that describes another thing, idea, or action in order to suggest a common quality shared by the two. Metaphors are often used in poetry and prose to create emphasis, variety, or new ideas and are implicit comparisons.

Example:

"Companies that smash the glass ceiling also enjoy higher profits, a new study indicates" ("Women and Profits," *Harvard Business Review* 79, no. 10 [November 2001]: 30).

Methods of Development: Organizational patterns used to structure the content. These include analysis, argument, cause-effect, chronology, classification, comparison-contrast, definition, description, enumeration, example, problem-solution, and process.

Parallelism: The use of the same or similar grammatical forms to express the same or similar ideas.

Example:

"In the process of publicly voicing problems, owning them, and fixing them, we grew more powerful, nimble, and tough-minded. In the course of becoming comfortable with honesty, we learned to respond quickly to internal and external changes" (Ginger L. Graham, "If You Want Honesty, Break Some Rules," *Harvard Business Review* 80, no. 4 [April 2002]: 47).

Paraphrase: A rewording or restatement of an author's meaning.

Purpose Statement: A statement of intention found in the abstract and introduction of a research paper or report; it announces the topic and tells readers why the document is being written. It is also used as a pre-writing technique to help writers clarify their purpose.

Report: A written document that contains an objective presentation of the facts of an investigation; an organized presentation of data, serving a practical purpose by supplying needed information.

Research Paper: A lengthy paper based on research and using numerous sources to answer a specific question, support a thesis, or prove a hypothesis.

Simile: A figure of speech in which one thing is compared to another dissimilar thing by the use of *like* or *as*. Similes are common in both poetry and prose. They differ from metaphors in being more explicit.

Example:

"Compaq is like a 6-foot-4-inch center in the National Basketball Association: the smallest big man in the league" (Randall E. Stross, "Can This Marriage Be Saved?" *U.S. News & World Report,* December 17, 2001, 41).

Style: The writer's manner of expression in language; the way of using words to express thoughts.

Summary: A brief restatement of the main ideas and major points of a longer written document, usually paraphrased.

Synthesis: An essay that is developed from two or more sources from which the writer selects information to support a thesis.

Thesis: The main idea of a text, expressed as a sentence; a statement assumed as a premise in a research paper, essay, argument, critical review, or synthesis.

Tone: A manner of writing that shows the attitude of the writer toward the subject and audience and results from word choice, sentence structure, and phrasing.

Topic Sentence: A sentence that contains the main idea of a paragraph and is often the first or last sentence of a paragraph.

Examples of Writing Styles

Subjective: I came to study in the United States in the fall of 2003 after graduating from my high school in Ankara, Turkey. I chose Washington, D.C., having heard that the city was beautiful, full of cultural attractions, and had an international population. When I first arrived at Georgetown University, located in northwest Washington, I was excited and happy to be starting a new and independent life. However, after about one month, culture shock affected me because I had trouble communicating in English, I couldn't adjust to American college life, and the liberal attitudes of Americans made me feel uncomfortable. ("My Experience with Culture Shock")

Objective: In the article "Other People's Words" (*Smithsonian*, March 2002), Paul Gray argues that even when plagiarism is not done intentionally, it remains an immoral act, and, therefore, should not be downplayed. Teachers may be confronted with students who plagiarize because they have not learned the rule about inserting quotation marks when using someone else's language. However, well-known authors who should know better also plagiarize other people's material, which is unethical and unacceptable behavior, according to Gray. (Olivier Cavagna, "Other People's Words")

Formal: The world community has a moral obligation to help poor nations achieve better health care. Improving health services in developing countries by donating an additional $27 billion per year by 2007 will not only be beneficial from a humanitarian view but will also help economically. It will save about 8 million lives annually and will also save $186 billion each year (Tyson 20). Unfortunately, these goals appear problematic due to a variety of reasons. Although this target represents an important opportunity for the entire world community, it is an extremely difficult goal to achieve and will require international cooperation. (Maimouna Ango, "Health and Wealth")

Informal: After I came to the States, it's true that my eating habits changed. I can't eat Latin American foods, my favorite foods I ate everyday in Colombia. I really miss the fresh fruits and vegetables from my country. But I can eat many different kinds of foods. And I have flexibility and curiosity about all foods because I like eating. In the United States, I can choose from a lot of stuff, so I think about what's good for my health. I guess it's important to pay attention to nutrition, no matter where I am. If I can do it, I'll stay healthy while I'm living here.

Business: It has come to my attention that many ITC employees are arriving late to work or are leaving early. This unauthorized change in the work schedule has had a negative impact on productivity and is against company policy. All employees must conform to the standard work schedule. Thank you for your cooperation on this critical issue.

Academic: "There have been times in the history of science when the whole of orthodox science has been rightly thrown over because of a single awkward fact. It would be arrogant to assert that such overthrows will never happen again. But we naturally, and rightly, demand a higher standard of authentication before accepting a fact that would turn a major and successful scientific edifice upside down, than before accepting a fact which, even if surprising, is readily accommodated by existing science." (Richard Dawkins, *The Blind Watchmaker: Why the Evidence of Evolution Reveals a Universe without Design* [New York and London: W. W. Norton & Company, 1996], 293)

Technical: "It has been shown convincingly that the feeling of thirst is associated with significant changes of activity in the cingulate cortex and in the insular cortex. The state of thirst itself results from detecting a water imbalance and from the subtle interplay between hormones such as vasopressin and angiotensin II and regions of the brain such as the hypothalamus and the periaqueductal gray, whose job it is to call into action thirst-relief behaviors, a collection of highly coordinated hormonal releases and motor programs." (Antonio Damasio, *Looking for Spinoza: Joy, Sorrow, and the Feeling Brain* [New York: Harcourt, Inc., 2003], 104)

Non-technical: Research shows that when a person feels thirsty, his or her brain activity in the cortex changes. Feelings of thirst result when certain hormones and parts of the brain cause the body to detect a water imbalance.

Conversational: "In the hills above Olympia, I awoke before dawn, feeling bleary-eyed from the Greek wine I'd drunk with some rowdy archeologists the night before. It was going to be a perfect summer day: from my hotel window I could see clear sky over the mountains of Arcadia, whose peaks covered the horizon like the waves of a wild blue sea. I needed some exercise—a jog to clear my head.

But where should I run in this corner of the rural Peloponnese? Where else, it occurred to me, but in the ancient Olympic Stadium?" (Tony Perrottet, "Let the Games Begin," *Smithsonian*, August 2004, 55)

Journalistic: "Remarkably, xerography was conceived by one person—Chester Carlson, a shy, soft-spoken patent attorney, who grew up in almost unspeakable poverty and worked his way through junior college and the California Institute of Technology. He made his discovery in solitude in 1937 and offered it to more than 20 major corporations, among them IBM, General Electric, Eastman Kodak and RCA. All of them turned him down, expressing what he later called 'an enthusiastic lack of interest' and thereby passing up the opportunity to manufacture what *Fortune* magazine would describe as 'the most successful product ever marketed in America.'" (David Owen, "Making Copies," *Smithsonian*, August 2004, 92)

Colorful: "Consider the following four dead-end kids. One was spanked by his teachers for bad grades and a poor attitude. He dropped out of school at 16. Another failed remedial English and came perilously close to flunking out of college. The third feared he'd never make it through school—and might not have without a tutor. The last finally learned to read in third grade, devouring Marvel comics, whose pictures provided clues to help him untangle the words.

"These four losers are, respectively, Richard Branson, Charles Schwab, John Chambers, and David Boies. Billionaire Branson developed one of Britain's top brands with Virgin Records and Virgin Atlantic Airways. Schwab virtually created the discount brokerage business. Chambers is CEO of Cisco. Boies is a celebrated trial attorney, best known as the guy who beat Microsoft." (Betsy Morris, "Overcoming Dyslexia," *Fortune*, May 13, 2002, 55–56)

Idiomatic: "Once you have earned credibility and are in a position to get what you want, you need to strike a series of devil's bargains. To horse-trade with the devil, you have to look him squarely in the eye and make the right demands from him. The deal I struck was to trade on my success as an actor in order to make films that otherwise wouldn't have been made because the studios thought they were not commercially viable." ("Turning an Industry Inside Out: A Conversation with Robert Redford," *Harvard Business Review* 80, no. 5 [May 2002]: 59)

Pictorial: "In big businesses, when you need to cross a river, you simply design a bridge, build it, and march right across. But in a small venture, you must climb on the rocks. You don't know exactly where each step will take you, but you do know the general direction you're moving in. If you make a mistake, you get wet. If your calculations are wrong, you have to inch your way back to safety and find a different route. And, as you jump from rock to rock, you have to *like* the feeling." (Dan Bricklin, "Natural-Born Entrepreneur," *Harvard Business Review* 79, no. 8 [September 2001]: 53–59)

Literary: "It was later, much later, when the need to return was upon me and I yearned for the great, cool hall of our house in Tawasi, for the smell of the fields and the black, starry night of the countryside before the High Dam brought electricity to the villages—when I yearned for Cairo, for Abu el-'Ela bridge, for the feel of the dust gritty under my fingers as I trailed my hand along the iron railing, for the smell of salted fish that met you as you drew near to Fasakhani Abu el-'Ela, for the sight of fruit piled high in symmetrical pyramids outside a greengrocer's shop and the twist of the brown paper bag in which you carry the fruit home, when I yearned even for the khamaseen winds that make you cover your face against the dust and with bowed head hurry quickly home—it was only then that I understood how longing for a place can take you over so that you can do nothing except return. . . ." (Ahdaf Soueif, *The Map of Love* [New York: Anchor Books, 2000], 119)

Poetic: "What she misses here is slow twilight, the sound of familiar trees. All through her youth in Toronto she learned to read the summer night. It was where she could be herself, lying in a bed, stepping onto a fire escape half asleep with a cat in her arms." (Michael Ondaatje, *The English Patient* [New York: Random House, 1993], 49)

Sentence Connectors

Addition
moreover, furthermore, in addition, also, then again, above all, likewise, similarly, again

Conclusion
finally, last, in conclusion, to conclude, altogether, overall, in general, in short, to summarize, to sum up

Contrast
however, nevertheless, nonetheless, conversely, on the other hand, on the contrary, rather, in contrast, in comparison

Enumeration
first, second, third, in the first place, in the second place, in the third place, then, next, finally, last, in conclusion, to conclude

Explanation
for example, for instance, in fact, indeed, namely, in other words, that is, to be specific, as a matter of fact, incidentally

Intensification
as a matter of fact, in fact, indeed, actually, on the contrary, surprisingly

Result
consequently, as a result, hence, therefore, thus, accordingly, for this reason

Transition
now, recently, eventually, overall, in general, generally, anyway, by the way, as we can see, in any case, of course

Punctuation Rules for Sentence Connectors

When you are using **conjunctive adverbs** as sentence connectors, be sure to punctuate them correctly. The punctuation for these sentence connectors is seen in these models.

Tomas is studying Italian**; moreover,** he is planning to spend a semester in Rome.

Tomas is studying Italian**. Moreover,** he is planning to spend a semester in Rome.

Tomas is studying Italian; he is**, moreover,** planning to spend a semester in Rome.

Tomas is studying Italian. He is**, moreover,** planning to spend a semester in Rome.

We will spend our vacation doing research, **and** we will write the report when we return.

When using **coordinate conjunctions** to connect two independent clauses, you should insert a comma before the following conjunctions: **and, but, for, nor, or, so, as, yet.**

The Power Writing Process

THE SUMMARY

I. **P**repare
   A. Complete the Author's Framework Form.
   B. Read the text quickly, looking for major points.
   C. Reread the text carefully. Underline or highlight the author's main idea, major points, and key supporting data.
   D. Reread the underlined or highlighted statements.

II. **O**utline
   A. Write one sentence expressing the main idea of the text you read.
   B. Add three or four major points and supporting data.
   C. Arrange the major points in logical order.
   D. Write a topic sentence for each major point.

III. **W**rite
   A. Using your outline, write a rough draft.
   B. In the first paragraph, give the author, title, source, date, and the main idea of the text.
   C. Paraphrase the author's words; do not copy directly from the text. However, you may include a few short quotations.
   D. Write in a clear, concise, and objective style.
   E. Do not add any extraneous information or give your opinion.

IV. **E**dit
   A. Be certain that the content of the summary is accurate and coherent.
   B. Delete any unnecessary information from the summary.
   C. Add information if the meaning is not clear and complete.
   D. Rearrange the information if the organization is not logical.
   E. Follow quotations with in-text citation of the author's last name and the page number (Johnson 125).

V. **R**ewrite
   A. Write the summary again, making the editorial changes.
   B. Proofread the summary for errors in grammar, punctuation, or spelling.
   C. Check the format for correct title, headings, spacing, and margins.
   D. Make all necessary corrections for the final copy of the summary.
   E. List your source as Works Cited at the end of the summary.

THE ESSAY

I. **P**repare
   A. Complete the Author's Framework Form.
   B. Collect and evaluate the information needed for the essay.
   C. Develop a tentative thesis (main idea) for the essay.

II. **O**utline
   A. Write a one-sentence thesis or main idea for the essay.
   B. Add three or four major points and supporting data.
   C. Arrange the major points in logical order.
   D. Write a topic sentence for each major point.

III. **W**rite
   A. Write the introduction to the essay, including the thesis (main idea).
   B. Write the body of the essay, following the outline and discussing each major point in a separate paragraph.
   C. Add supporting data (facts, examples, statistics, quotations) to the essay to support the major points.
   D. Cite your sources using in-text citation of the author's last name and the page number (Johnson 125).
   E. Write the conclusion to the essay by restating or paraphrasing your thesis and adding concluding data (summary, prediction, solution or quotation).

IV. **E**dit
   A. Check for accurate and coherent content in the essay.
   B. Check for logical and clear organization in the essay.
   C. Be certain that the essay is written in an academic style.
   D. Delete any unnecessary information from and add missing information to the essay.

V. **R**ewrite
   A. Write the essay again, making editorial changes.
   B. Proofread the essay for errors in grammar, punctuation, or spelling.
   C. Check the format for correct title, headings, spacing, and margins.
   D. Make all necessary corrections for the final copy of the essay.
   E. List your sources as Works Cited at the end of the essay. Alphabetize them by the authors' last names.

THE CRITICAL REVIEW

I. **P**repare
   A. Complete the Author's Framework Form.
   B. Read the text quickly, looking for the main argument and the major points.
   C. Reread the text carefully. Underline or highlight the author's argument, major points, and key supporting data.
   D. Decide on the criteria by which you will evaluate the author's ideas.

II. **O**utline
   A. Write a one-sentence thesis that is the foundation for the critical review.
   B. Write an outline of four sections, with major points and supporting data.
   C. Arrange the major points in logical order, beginning with the summary.
   D. Write a topic sentence for each major point.

III. **W**rite
   A. Write an introduction, including the title and author of the book or article and the thesis.
   B. Write the body of the critical review, following the outline and discussing each major point in a separate paragraph.
   C. Use brief quotations or paraphrased passages from the book or article to support the thesis, and cite your sources using in-text citation of the author's last name and the page number (Johnson 125).
   D. Write the conclusion to the critical review by restating or paraphrasing your thesis and adding concluding data (summary, prediction, solution, or quotation).

IV. **E**dit
   A. Check for accurate and coherent content in the critical review.
   B. Check for logical and clear organization in the critical review.
   C. Be certain that the critical review is written in a formal academic style.
   D. Be certain that the body paragraphs of the critical review support your thesis (your evaluation of the author's argument).

V. **R**ewrite
   A. Write the critical review again, making the editorial changes.
   B. Proofread the critical review for errors in grammar, punctuation, or spelling.
   C. Check the format for correct title, headings, spacing, and margins.
   D. Make all necessary corrections for the final copy of the critical review.
   E. List your sources as Works Cited at the end of the critical review. Alphabetize them by the authors' last names.

THE SYNTHESIS

I. **P**repare
  A. Complete the Author's Framework Form.
  B. Read the selections carefully, thinking about the authors' themes and main ideas.
  C. Develop a tentative thesis (main idea) that can be supported by all the readings. The thesis can be an argument or an analytical statement.
  D. Read the selections again, underlining the sentences that relate to your thesis.

II. **O**utline
  A. Write a one-sentence thesis that is the foundation for the synthesis.
  B. Add three or four major points and supporting data.
  C. Arrange the major points in logical order.
  D. Write a topic sentence for each major point.

III. **W**rite
  A. Write an introduction for the synthesis, including your sources (authors, titles, sources, dates), a brief summary of the sources, and thesis.
  B. Write the body of the synthesis, following the outline and discussing each major point in a separate paragraph.
  C. Use brief quotations or paraphrased passages from the readings to support the thesis, and cite your sources using in-text citation of the author's last name and the page number (Johnson 125).
  D. Write the conclusion to the synthesis by restating or paraphrasing your thesis and adding concluding data (summary, prediction, solution, or quotation).

IV. **E**dit
  A. Check for accurate and coherent content in the synthesis.
  B. Check for logical and clear organization in the synthesis.
  C. Be certain that the synthesis is written in a formal academic style
  D. Be certain that the body paragraphs support your thesis.

V. **R**ewrite
  A. Write the synthesis again, making the editorial changes.
  B. Proofread the synthesis for errors in grammar, punctuation, or spelling.
  C. Check the format for correct title, headings, spacing, and margins.
  D. Make all necessary corrections for the final copy of the synthesis.
  E. List your sources as Works Cited at the end of the synthesis. Alphabetize them by the authors' last names.

THE ARGUMENT

I. **P**repare
   A. Complete the Author's Framework Form.
   B. Read books or articles about your topic.
   C. Think about the various issues involved in the topic.

II. **O**utline
   A. Write a one-sentence thesis that is the foundation for the argument.
   B. Add two major points supporting your thesis, one major point containing a refutation of the counter-argument and a conclusion.
   C. Arrange the major points in logical order.
   D. Write a topic sentence for each major point.

III. **W**rite
   A. Write an introduction, including background information and the thesis.
   B. Write the body of the argument, following the outline and discussing each major point in a separate paragraph.
   C. Use brief quotations or paraphrased passages from books or articles to support the thesis, and cite your sources using in-text citation of the author's last name and the page number (Johnson 125).
   D. Write the conclusion to the argument by restating or paraphrasing your thesis and adding concluding data (summary, prediction, solution, or quotation).

IV. **E**dit
   A. Check for accurate and coherent content in the argument.
   B. Check for logical and clear organization in the argument.
   C. Be certain that the argument is written in a formal academic style.
   D. Be certain that the body paragraphs of the argument support your thesis (your evaluation of the author's ideas).

V. **R**ewrite
   A. Write the argument again, making the editorial changes.
   B. Proofread the argument for errors in grammar, punctuation, or spelling.
   C. Check the format for correct title, headings, spacing, and margins.
   D. Make all necessary corrections for the final copy of the argument.
   E. List your sources as Works Cited at the end of the argument. Alphabetize them by the authors' last names.

APPENDIX E

Writing Evaluation Forms

Summary Evaluation

Evaluator _____

Author _____

Excellent +	**Satisfactory √**	**Unsatisfactory –**

Content
- Main idea _____
- Major points _____

Organization
- Main idea in paragraph 1 _____
- Paragraph coherence _____

Style
- Accurate paraphrasing _____
- Use of quotations _____

Mechanics
- Standard English grammar _____
- Punctuation, capitalization, spelling _____

Format
- Author, title, source, date in paragraph 1 _____
- Paragraphing _____

Overall Evaluation _____

Comments

Essay Evaluation

Evaluator _____
Author _____

Excellent +	Satisfactory √	Unsatisfactory –

Content
- Appropriate thesis _____
- Logical development _____
- Relevant information _____

Organization
- Thesis in paragraph 1 _____
- Topic sentences _____
- Paragraph and essay coherence _____

Style
- Academic style _____
- Use of quotations _____
- Clarity, conciseness, precision _____

Mechanics
- Standard English grammar _____
- Punctuation, capitalization, spelling _____
- Citation of sources _____

Format
- Margins and spacing _____
- 12-point font _____
- Paragraphing _____

Overall Evaluation _____

Comments

Critical Review Evaluation

Evaluator _____
Author   _____

Excellent +   **Satisfactory √**   **Unsatisfactory –**

Content
- Logic of introduction and thesis   _____
- Support for thesis   _____
- Analysis of author's ideas   _____

Organization
- Thesis in paragraph 1   _____
- Topic sentences   _____
- Paragraph and essay coherence   _____

Style
- Paraphrasing   _____
- Use of quotations   _____
- Clarity, conciseness, precision   _____

Mechanics
- Standard English grammar   _____
- Punctuation, capitalization, spelling   _____
- Citation of sources   _____

Format
- Author, title, source, date in paragraph 1 _____
- Paragraphing   _____
- Works Cited at end of critical review   _____

Overall Evaluation _____

Comments

Synthesis Evaluation

Evaluator _____
Author _____

Excellent +   **Satisfactory √**   **Unsatisfactory –**

Content
- Logic of introduction and thesis   _____
- Support for thesis   _____
- Balanced use of sources   _____

Organization
- Thesis in paragraph 1   _____
- Topic sentences   _____
- Paragraph and essay coherence   _____

Style
- Paraphrasing   _____
- Use of quotations   _____
- Clarity, conciseness, precision   _____

Mechanics
- Standard English grammar   _____
- Punctuation, capitalization, spelling   _____
- Citation of sources   _____

Format
- Authors, titles, sources, dates in paragraph 1   _____
- Paragraphing   _____
- Works Cited at end of synthesis   _____

Overall Evaluation _____

Comments

Argument Evaluation

Evaluator _____
Author   _____

Excellent +	Satisfactory √	Unsatisfactory −

Content
- Logic of introduction and thesis   _____
- Analysis of author's ideas   _____
- Support for thesis   _____
- Effective refutation   _____

Organization
- Thesis in paragraph 1   _____
- Topic sentences   _____
- Paragraph and essay coherence   _____

Style
- Paraphrasing   _____
- Use of quotations   _____
- Clarity, conciseness, precision   _____

Mechanics
- Standard English grammar   _____
- Punctuation, capitalization, spelling   _____
- Citation of sources   _____

Format
- Author, title, source, date in paragraph 1   _____
- Paragraphing   _____
- Works Cited at end of argument   _____

Overall Evaluation _____

Comments

Research Paper Evaluation

Evaluator _____

Author   _____

Excellent +	Satisfactory √	Unsatisfactory −

Content
- Proof of argument   _____
- Logic of development   _____
- Synthesis of information   _____

Organization
- Thesis in introduction   _____
- Topic sentences   _____
- Paragraph and paper coherence   _____

Style
- Paraphrasing   _____
- Use of quotations   _____
- Clarity, conciseness, precision   _____

Mechanics
- Standard English grammar   _____
- Punctuation, capitalization, spelling   _____
- Citation of sources   _____

Format
- Paragraphing   _____
- Spacing and margins   _____
- Page numbers   _____

Documentation
- Form of citations   _____
- Number of citations   _____
- Works Cited   _____

Overall Evaluation _____

Comments

Peer Critique

Evaluator _____

Author _____

Use this form when you evaluate your classmate's writing assignment. Mark the document as Excellent (E), Satisfactory (S), or Unsatisfactory (U) in each of these categories:

- Grammar   correct standard English   _____

- Mechanics   correct punctuation, capitalization, and spelling   _____

- Organization   logical and coherent development of ideas   _____

- Content   substantive, meaningful, relevant discussion of the topic   _____

- Format   appropriate and consistent presentation on the page   _____

- Documentation   accurate and sufficient citation of sources   _____

Overall Evaluation _____

Suggestions and Comments

_____

_____

_____

_____

_____

_____

Internet Research

This text requires the use of outside sources for many assignments, including sources found on the Internet. Thus, it is important for you to be able to use the Internet in the most efficient manner. This information will help you to search for and access websites. Since every library has its own system of organization, you should become familiar with your library system and its e-resource collection. In addition, you should become adept at evaluating Internet sources to determine their value and validity. Duke University provides an excellent explanation of how to evaluate websites: *www.lib.duke.edu/libguide/home.htm*.

--------------------------------- **THE INTERNET** ---------------------------------

Search Engines

Many different search engines can be used to locate a book, journal, or newspaper article, or just to find information on a topic. Before using these search engines, take time to read their Help screens. The most comprehensive search engine currently is Google™ *(www.google.com)*. The search engines that follow are also available.

AltaVista™: *www.altavista.digital.com*
Excite®: *http://my.excite.com*
HotBot®: *www.hotbot.lycos.com*
Lycos: *www.lycos.com*
WebCrawler®: *www.webcrawler.com*
Yahoo!®: *www.yahoo.com*

Resources Available on the Internet

- **Almanacs**
  Infoplease®: *www.infoplease.com*

- **Country studies**
  The Central Intelligence Agency, The World Factbook: *www.cia.gov*
  The Library of Congress: *www.loc.gov*
  United Nations: *www.un.org*
  The World Bank Group: *www.worldbank.org/*

- **Encyclopedias**
  Encyclopaedia Britannica Online: *www.britannica.com/*
  MSN Learning and Research (Click Encyclopedia): *http://encarta. msn.com*
  Smithsonian (Click Research and check the many resources available): *www.si.edu*

- **Online news sites**
  AlterNet: *www.alternet.org/*
  British Broadcasting Company: *www.bbc.co.uk/*
  BusinessWeek: *www.businessweek.com*
  Cable News Network: *www.cnn.com/*
  The Christian Science Monitor: *www.csmonitor.com*
  Financial Times: *http://news.ft.com/home/us*
  Fortune: *www.fortune.com/fortune/*
  MSNBC News: *www.msnbc.com*
  The New York Times: *www.nytimes.com/*
  Time: *www.time.com/time/*
  Salon.com: *www.salon.com*
  Slate: *www.slate.msn.com/*
  USA Today: *www.usatoday.com/*
  The Wall Street Journal: *http://online.wsj.com*
  The Washington Post: *www.washingtonpost.com/*
  Wired News: *www.wired.com*
  WorldPress.org: *www.worldpress.org*
  Yahoo!® News: *http:// news.yahoo.com*

─────────── **ACADEMIC RESOURCES** ───────────

Library Electronic Access to Resource Material (E-Resource Collection)

Libraries offer online databases that allow students and professors to conduct research over the Internet from their homes, offices, or dorm rooms. These databases provide an array of information, from library holdings of books and journals to statistics and company data, and the full text of journal and newspaper articles. Some academic journals, such as the *Harvard Business Review* and the *Sloan Management Review*, only provide article abstracts to most databases. To read the full text of an article, you must go to the library and find the issue of the print journal in which it was originally published.

- **Specialized databases for business and economics that provide the full text of many articles**
  ABI/Inform
  LexisNexis Academic
  Business and Company Resource Center
  Business Source

- **Databases for journal articles**
  ProQuest General Reference
  InfoTrac
  EBSCO Academic

- **Selected journals that provide the full text of articles online through databases**
  BusinessWeek
  Computerworld
  The Economist
  Forbes
  Foreign Policy
  Fortune
  Harvard International Review
  Newsweek
  Time

Note: Changes often occur in Internet addresses (URLs) and online resources. Please visit *www.press.umich.edu/esl/* to monitor changes to the URLs or online resources printed in this book. To notify us of changes, e-mail *esladmin@umich.edu*.

"My Healthy Lifestyle" Revision (pages 49–50)

(Changes are in bold.)

Living in Washington, DC, is different **from living** in Colombia in many ways. Actually, I try to **live a healthy life** everyday. Fortunately, **in Washington, I can walk to** many excellent inexpensive restaurants and sightseeing places and **museums,** so I have **the** opportunity to eat **delicious meals** and to exercise. **Furthermore, I try** not to eat too **much food with fat and sugar**. Of course, sometimes **this** is difficult to do since fast food **restaurants like** McDonalds are everywhere I look. **Nevertheless, since I have been in Washington, DC, my lifestyle has been generally healthy with regard to my diet, but I exercised more in Colombia than I do here.**

After I came to the United States, it is true that my eating **habits changed**. I no longer eat **my favorite Latin American food** that I **ate** everyday in Colombia. **I really miss** the fresh fruits and vegetables from my country. **However,** I eat many **different kinds of food,** and I am flexible and curious about **all** food **because** I enjoy eating very much. In the United States, I can choose from a **large assortment of items.** Thus, I **think** about what is good for my health. I guess it **is** important to pay attention **to** nutrition, no matter where I am. If I can do it, I **will stay** healthy while **living** here.

On the other hand, it is difficult for me to exercise **because** I don't like the cold weather and, in fact, I don't have as much time to exercise as **I had** in Colombia. But since I like walking, I **sometimes** walk between the Roslyn metro station and the university. Although this is only a small **activity,** I think **it** is more helpful for my health to do something than **to** do nothing. In addition, **on weekends,** I often walk around Washington, which is a beautiful city, **so I get some exercise.** For example, last weekend I **walked** from the Lincoln Memorial to the Washington Monument.

I really enjoy my life in Washington, DC, and I **have adjusted** to this new culture **quite** well. **Moreover,** I would like to take advantage **of** the rest of my stay **here;** therefore, I plan to **continue my healthy lifestyle** until I **go** back to Colombia. No matter where I am living, thinking about diet and nutrition **is** important, **and** exercising should also be a priority.

Bibliography and Suggested Reading

Bates, Jefferson D. *Writing with Precision: How to Write So That You Cannot Possibly Be Misunderstood.* New York: Penguin Group USA, 2000.

Bernstein, Theodore M. *The Careful Writer: A Modern Guide to English Usage.* New York: Athaneum, 1984.

Damasio, Antonio. *Looking for Spinoza: Joy, Sorrow, and the Feeling Brain.* New York: Harcourt, Inc., 2003.

Dawkins, Richard. *The Blind Watchmaker: Why the Evidence of Evolution Reveals a Universe without Design.* New York: W. W. Norton, 1996.

———. *River Out of Eden: A Darwinian View of Life.* New York: HarperCollins, 1995.

Dillard, Annie. *An American Childhood.* New York: HarperCollins, 1987.

Fowler, H. W. *A Dictionary of Modern English Usage.* New York: Crown Publishers, 1983.

Gibaldi, Joseph. *MLA Handbook for Writers of Research Papers. 6th ed.* New York: MLA, 2003.

Miller, Casey, and Kate Swift. *The Handbook of Nonsexist Writing.* New York: Lippincott & Crowell, 1980.

Palmquist, Mike. *The Bedford Researcher: An Integrated Text, CD-ROM, and Web Site.* New York: Bedford/St. Martin's, 2003.

Sora, Joseph W., ed. *Random House Writer's Reference.* New York: Random House, 2003.

Strunk, William, Jr., and E. B. White. *The Elements of Style. 4th ed.* New York: Longman, 2000.

Swales, John M., and Christine B. Feak. *Academic Writing for Graduate Students. 2nd ed.* Ann Arbor: University of Michigan Press, 2004.

Truss, Lynne. *Eats, Shoots & Leaves: The Zero Tolerance Approach to Punctuation.* New York: Gotham Books, 2004.

Williams, William Carlos, et al. *The Collected Poems of William Carlos Williams: 1909–1939*. Vol. 1. New York: New Directions, 1995.

———. *The Collected Poems of William Carlos Williams: 1939–1962*. Vol. 2. New York: New Directions, 2001.

Zinsser, William. *On Writing Well: The Classic Guide to Writing Nonfiction, 25th Anniversary Edition*. New York: HarperCollins, 2001.